D0931543

George Washington Carver

-His life & faith in his own words-

By
William J. Federer

George Washington Carver

-His life & faith in his own words-

By
William J. Federer

Library of Congress
HISTORY / INSPIRATION   ISBN 0-9653557-6-4   UPC 82189800008
Photographs of George Washington Carver courtesy of
Tuskegee University Archives
Special Collections of Iowa State University Library
Simpson College Archives, Dunn Library, Indianola, IA
George Washington Carver National Monument

Amerisearch, Inc., P.O. Box 20163, St. Louis, MO 63123, 1-888-USA-WORD
314-487-4395 voice/fax, www.amerisearch.net, wjfederer@aol.com

In memory of

my grandparents

Orval and Therese Epperson

(1891-1976), (1893-1991)

of

Neosho, Missouri,

who gave me my first book

on

George Washington Carver

when I was a young boy.

Contents

Contents

Foreword

So often, authors are the privileged ones, experiencing the adventure of reading through an individual's personal manuscripts, papers and correspondence when compiling biographies. They uncover little known details, examine unpublished documents, formulate opinions and write their conclusions in a book for readers to peruse. Invariably, the author cannot help but shade his or her conclusions with some of their own views.

Being that a person's faith is possibly the most intimate aspect of their life, this author has decided the most unbiased way to explore the faith that motivated and guided George Washington Carver is to allow you to partake in the adventure of an author, examining for yourself letters to his dearest friends, notes to his closest associates and correspondence to those who played pivotal roles in his life.

Together, we can discover the intimate side of this great man who touched millions around the world. Join me the adventure of meeting George Washington Carver by reading his life and faith *in his own words.*

George Washington Carver
Iowa State Graduation Portrait, 1894

Introduction
Humble Birth – Noble Work

George Washington Carver was an African American chemist of international fame in the field of agriculture. He introduced hundreds of uses for the peanut, soybean, pecan and sweet potato, which revolutionized the economy of the South by creating a market for these products. These crops also replenished the soil which had been depleted through years of cotton growth. By the early 1940's, George's agricultural contributions had resulted in peanut farming covering over 5 million acres, with over $500,000,000 in peanut industry production. But life did not start out easy for this scientist.

George was born a slave during the Civil War, possibly in 1865, but there are no records. Within a few weeks, his father, who belonged to the next farm over, was killed in a log hauling accident. Shortly after the War, while still an infant, George, with his mother and sister, were kidnapped by bushwhackers. Moses Carver sent friends to track down the thieves and trade his best horse to retrieve them. The thieves took the horse and only left George, lying on the ground, sick with the whooping cough. George never saw his mother and sister again. Meanwhile, illness claimed the lives of his two other sisters and they were buried on the Carver farm.

George and his older brother, Jim, were raised in Diamond Grove, Missouri, by Uncle Moses and Aunt Sue Carver, an elderly white couple who never had children. Being of poor health as a child, George spent much time around the house helping with chores, learning to cook, clean, sew, mend, and do laundry. His recreation was to spend time in the woods near the house.

Around the age of ten, George said goodbye to the Carvers and walked the eight miles to Neosho, Missouri, to attend school. By chance, he was taken in by Uncle Andy and Aunt Mariah Watkins, a childless African American couple who treated him as their own. George paid his tuition and helped with the finances by working odd jobs around

Aunt Mariah Watkins, with local children. She and Uncle Andy Watkins took George Carver in when he came to Neosho as a boy.

town, such as cooking, weeding, grooming horses, chopping wood, sewing, mending and doing laundry. Aunt Mariah gave George a Bible which he cherished dearly.

After learning all he could from Schoolmaster Foster, George decided to hitch a ride with a family traveling to Fort Scott, Kansas, where he boarded in a lean-to behind the stagecoach depot, then later under the back steps of a home. He worked as a cook and attended school, but fled suddenly after witnessing a lynching.

Carver continued through school in Oletha, Kansas, then at Paola Normal School, finishing High School in Minneapolis, Kansas. There he received the sad news that his only brother, Jim, had died of small pox.

George attended a business college in Kansas City, where he learned shorthand and typing, and worked as a stenographer for the Union Telegraph Office. He applied and was accepted at Highland College, but was refused entrance because of his race.

Discouraged, he headed to Ness County in Western Kansas, where he tried his hand at homesteading. The county folks quickly accepted George, admiring this gentle black man who played accordion at their dances, joined their literary societies and impressed them with his paintings.

George's memories and correspondence with the people there remained precious to him throughout his life, as did the invaluable experience of learning to farm.

George then worked as the head cook at a large hotel in Winterset, Iowa. While attending church there, he met John and Helen Milholland, who encouraged him to continue his education, pursuing art and music at Simpson College in Indianola, Iowa. One of his paintings, *The Yucca,* received an Honorable Mention at the 1893 Chicago World's Fair. In order to support himself, he opened a laundry service for the other students.

His art teacher, Miss Etta M. Budd, noticed how intricately he painted plants and encouraged him to study agriculture. He transferred

George W. Carver's paintings, The Yucca, *received an Honorable Mention at the 1893 Chicago World's Fair.*

Miss Etta M. Budd was George Carver's art teacher at Simpson College.

to Iowa State College of Agriculture and Mechanical Arts. Student living quarters became crowded and before Carver's race could be made an issue, the head of the Agricultural Department, Professor James Wilson, let Carver board in his office.

George received his bachelors degree from Iowa State in 1894, masters degree in 1896, and accepted a prestigious faculty position there.

Two of Carver's professors, James Wilson and Henry C. Wallace, served as U.S. Secretary of Agriculture, and one of his students, Henry A. Wallace, became U.S. Secretary of Agriculture and Vice President under Franklin D. Roosevelt.

In the spring of 1896, George W. Carver received a letter from Booker T. Washington, president of the Tuskegee Institute in Alabama:

> Tuskegee Institute seeks to provide education - a means for survival to those who attend. Our students are poor, often starving. They travel miles of torn roads, across years of poverty. We teach them to read and write, but words cannot fill stomachs. They need to learn how to plant and harvest crops....
>
> I cannot offer you money, position or fame. The first two you have. The last, from the place you now occupy, you will no doubt achieve.
>
> These things I now ask you to give up. I offer you in their place - work - hard, hard work - the challenge of bringing people from degradation, poverty and waste to full manhood.
>
> Booker T. Washington [1]

Booker T. Washington invited Carver to join the Tuskegee Institute staff.

On May 16, 1896, George W. Carver responded to Booker T. Washington:

My dear Sir,

I am just in receipt of yours of the 13th inst., and hasten to reply.

I am looking forward to a very busy, pleasant and profitable time at your college and shall be glad to cooperate with you in doing all I can through Christ who strengtheneth me to better the condition of our people.

Some months ago I read your stirring address delivered at Chicago and I said amen to all you said, furthermore you have the correct solution to the "race problem".... Providence permitting, I will be there in Nov.

God bless you and your work,

Geo. W. Carver [2]

In the fall of 1896, George surprised the staff at Iowa State College by announcing his plans to give up his promising future there and join the Tuskegee Institute in Alabama. The staff showed their appreciation by purchasing him a going away present, a microscope, which he used extensively throughout his career.

George assembled an Agricultural Department at Tuskegee, and would go out among the farmers, teaching them good farming techniques, such as crop rotation, fertilization and erosion prevention. He noticed that the soil was depleted due to years of repeated cotton growth and produced very poorly. Not too long after this, an insect, the boll weevil, swept through the South, destroying cotton crops and leaving farmers devastated.

George showed the farmers the benefits of planting legumes, such as peanuts, which replenish the soil with nitrogen. The farmers heeded his advice but soon had more peanuts than the market wanted, as peanuts were primarily used as feed for farm animals.

George went into his laboratory, determined to find more uses for the peanut so that there would be a bigger market for the southern farmers. He discovered over three hundred uses for the peanut, over one hundred eighteen for the sweet potato, over sixty for the pecan, as well as dozens more for the soybean, cowpea, wild plum, okra, etc. A partial list, compiled by the Carver Museum, includes:

Iowa State

Microscope given to Carver from Iowa State

*BEVERAGES: blackberry punch, cherry punch, lemon punch, orange punch,

Southern Cotton fields

Bales of Cotton on Southern Wharf

George Washington Carver - His Life & Faith in His Own Words

peanut punch, beverage for ice cream, evaporated peanut beverage; dry coffee, instant coffee, 32 different kinds of milk, dehydrated milk flakes, buttermilk;

*FOODS: peanut butter, salted peanuts, peanut flour, peanut flakes, peanut meal, cream from peanut milk, butter from peanut milk, egg yolk, breakfast food, bisque powder, cheese, cream cheese, cheese pimento, cheese sandwich, cheese tutti frutti, cocoa, crystallized peanuts, curds, granulated potatoes, potato nibs, golden nuts, mock coconut, pancake flour, peanut hearts, peanut surprise, peanut wafers, pickle, sweet pickle, shredded peanuts, substitute asparagus;

*MEATS SUBSTITUTES: mock meat, mock chicken, mock goose, mock veal cutlet, mock oyster, peanut sausage;

*SAUCES & INGREDIENTS: chili sauce, chop suey sauce, Worcestershire sauce, vinegar, spiced vinegar, salad oil, cooking oil, oleomargarine, mayonnaise, lard compound, molasses, malted substitutes, meat tenderizer, cheese nut sage, flavoring paste, peanut relish, peanut tofu sauce, starch, synthetic ginger, white pepper, yeast;

*CANDIES & DESSERTS: peanut brittle, bar candy, peanut and popcorn bars, caramel, chocolate, chocolate coated peanuts, peanut chocolate fudge, after dinner mints, lemon drops, orange drops, synthetic tapioca, sugar, cream candy, peanut cake, peanut dainties, peanut kisses;

*MEDICINES: castoria substitute, emulsion for bronchitis, goiter treatment, iron tonic, laxatives, medicine similar to castor oil, rubbing oil, tannic acid, quinine;

*COSMETICS: all purpose cream, face cream, vanishing cream, cold cream, shaving cream, baby massage cream, fat producing cream, face lotion, hand lotion, rubbing oil, oil for hair and scalp, peanut oil shampoo, face powder, talcum powder, antiseptic soap, toilet soap, face ointment, glycerine, tetter and dandruff cure, face bleach and tan remover;

*ANIMAL FEED & FARMING: hen food for laying, molasses feed, peanut hay meal, peanut hull meal, peanut hull bran, peanut meal, peanut stock food; hog feed, stock feed meal, fertilizer, soil conditioner, insecticides;

*DYES, PAINTS & STAINS: leather stains from mahogany to blue, wood stains, paints, shoe and leather blackening, shoe polish, metal polish, writer's ink, printer's ink, dyes for cloth, special peanut dye, non-toxic pigments from which crayons were eventually created;

*GENERAL: adhesives, alcohol, paper, rope, cordage, mats, synthetic cotton, synthetic silk, coke from hulls, plastics, synthetic rubber; lubricating oil, axle grease;

*SOAPS & DETERGENTS: laundry soap, sweeping compound, washing powder, soap stock, cleaner for hands, bleach;

*CONSTRUCTION: wall boards from peanut hulls, sizing for walls, carpet, linoleum, insulating boards, wood filler, synthetic marble, highway paving material, creosote, glue, nitroglycerine;

*FUEL: gas, gasoline, diesel fuel, illuminating oil, briquettes, charcoal from peanut shells.

Carver was recognized by both black and white leaders, and in 1918 he was appointed to the U.S. Department of Agriculture. In 1923, Joel Elias Springarn, a white publisher and former chairman of the board of the National Association for the Advancement of Colored People, awarded Carver the Springarn Medal for Distinguished Service in Agricultural Chemistry. Carver received an honorary doctorate from Simpson College in 1928, and was made a member of the Royal Society of London, England.

Henry Ford became personal friends with Dr. Carver, being fascinated with his method of deriving rubber from milkweed. Mr. Ford visited him twice at Tuskegee Institute and tried many times to persuade Dr. Carver to join him in business. Carver declined, being committed to helping his people in the South. Mr. Ford built a replica of Dr. Carver's birthplace at his *Dearborn Village,* and built a school for children named *George Washington Carver School.*

Henry Ford, friend of Dr. Carver's

In 1923, Vice-President Calvin Coolidge visited George Washington Carver at Tuskegee Institute, as did President Franklin D. Roosevelt later. Carver became a confidant and advisor to leaders and scientists from all over the world, ranging from Mohandas K. Gandhi to Thomas Edison. Edison offered him a six-figure income position at Menlo Park, but Carver turned it down. Even Josef Stalin invited him to come Russia in 1931.

Calvin Coolidge visited Carver at Tuskegee.

Dr. George W. Carver also made medical contributions, including using a combination of oil derived from peanuts, called Penol, together with physical therapy to restore the use of atrophied limbs of Polio and infantile paralysis victims.

George Washington Carver died on January 5, 1943. In July of that year, President Franklin D. Roosevelt dedicated Carver's birthplace in Diamond, Missouri, as a National Monument. This was the first National Monument to someone other than a United States President. Congress designated the date of his death as "George Washington Carver Day."

The U.S. Postal Service issued two stamps displaying his picture, January 5, 1948, and February 3, 1998. The U.S. Mint struck a fifty-cent coin with the images of George Washington Carver and Booker T. Washington.

In June 15, 1966, a nuclear submarine, 37th Fleet Ballistic Missile, was dedicated the U.S.S. George Washington Carver, with the motto "Strength through Knowledge."

George Washington Carver Stamps & Fifty-Cent Coin with Booker T. Washington

Henry A. Wallace (left) was a former student of Carver's who became U.S. Secretary of Agriculture and Vice President under President Franklin D. Roosevelt

Dr. Carver opening mail from around the world.

Nuclear Submarine U.S.S. George Washington Carver,
37th Fleet Ballistic Missile,
was commissioned June 15, 1966,
with the motto "Strength through Knowledge."

Chapter I - 1890-1891
Simpson College

In 1890, while a student at Simpson College, George W. Carver ended his letter to John and Helen Milholland:

> Nearly 12, please excuse me and write sooner than you did before. My best respects to all. I remain your humble servant of God. I am learning to trust and realize the blessed results from trusting in Him every day. I am glad to hear of your advancement spiritually and financially. I regard them also as especial blessings from God.
> Sincerely yours,
> Geo. W. Carver [3]

On April 8, 1890, George wrote from Simpson College to John and Helen Milholland of Winterset, Iowa:

> I am taking better care of myself than I have. I realize that God has a great work for me to do and consequently I must be very careful on my health. You will doubtless be surprised to learn that I am taking both vocal and instrumental music (piano) this term. I don't have to pay any direct money for any music, but pay it in paintings....
> I am glad the outlook for the upbuilding of the kingdom of Christ is so good. We are having a great revival here. 40 seeking last night and 25 arose for prayers at the close of the service... Shall be glad to hear from you soon.
> Geo. W. Carver [4]

Carver painting at Simpson College

Photograph courtesy of the Simpson College Archives, Indianola, IA

Photo courtesy of the Simpson College Archives, Indianola, IA

George Washington Carver National Monument, Diamond Grove, Missouri

George W. Carver as a young man.

Chapter II - 1891-1896
Iowa State College

On August 6, 1891, in his first letter to the Milhollands after enrolling at Iowa State College, George W. Carver wrote:

> I as yet do not like it as well here as I do at Simpson because the helpful means for a Christian growth is not so good; but the Lord helping me I will do the best I can....
>
> I am glad to hear that the work for Christ is progressing. Oh how I wish the people would awake up from their lethargy and come out soul and body for Christ.
>
> I am so anxious to get out and be doing something. I can hardly wait for the time to come. The more my ideas develop, the more beautiful and grand seems the plan I have laid out to pursue, or rather the one God has destined for me.
>
> It is really all I see in a successful life. And let us hope that in the mysterious ways of the Lord, he will bring about these things we all so much hope for. I wish it was so that we could assist each other in the work as there is such a sameness in it, and I seen by one of the late southern papers that one of their strongest men advocate a broader system of education, and lays down a plan very much like the one I have but not as broad.
>
> And the more I study and pray over it, the more I am convinced it is the right coarse to pursue.... Let us pray that the Lord will completely guide us in all things, and that we may gladly be led by Him.... My hope is still keeping without becoming stale either.
>
> George [5]

On October 15, 1894, George W. Carver wrote to John & Helen Milholland from Iowa State College:

My dear friends,
I am glad to know that you are all well and that the Lord is blessing you so unsparingly. Beg pardon for finishing with a pencil but my pen has run dry and I have no ink with which to fill it. The Lord is wonderfully blessing me and has for these many years. I cannot begin to tell you all I presume you know. I had some paintings at the Cedar Rapids Art exhibit, was there myself and had some work selected and sent to The World's Fair, was also sent to Lake Geneva twice to the Y.M.C.A as a representative from our college.

And the many good things the Lord has entrusted to my care are too numerous to mention here. The last but not least, I have been elected Assistant Station botanist. I intend to take a post graduate course here, which will take two years. One year of residence work and one nonresidence work. I hope to do my nonresidence work next year and in the meantime take a course at the Chicago academy of arts and Moody Institute. I am saving all the pennies I can for the purpose and am praying a great deal. I believe more and more in prayer all the time...
Geo. W. Carver [6]

Early 1896, Booker T. Washington, president of the Tuskegee Institute in Alabama, addressed the following letter to George W. Carver:

Tuskegee Institute seeks to provide education - a means for survival to those who attend. Our students are poor, often starving. They travel miles of torn roads, across years of poverty. We teach them to read and write, but words cannot fill stomachs. They need to learn how to plant and harvest crops....

I cannot offer you money, position or fame. The first two you have. The last, from the place you now occupy, you will no doubt achieve. These things I now ask you to give up.

I offer you in their place - work - hard, hard work - the challenge of bringing people from degradation, poverty and waste to full manhood.

Booker T. Washington [7]

On May 16, 1896, George W. Carver responded to Booker T. Washington:

My dear Sir,

I am just in receipt of yours of the 13th inst., and hasten to reply. I am looking forward to a very busy, pleasant and profitable time at your college and shall be glad to cooperate with you in doing all I can through Christ who strengtheneth me to better the condition of our people.

Some months ago I read your stirring address delivered at Chicago and I said amen to all you said, furthermore you have the correct solution to the "race problem".... Providence permitting, I will be there in Nov. God bless you and your work,

Geo. W. Carver [8]

George Washington Carver (left) examining plants with a student, c1900

Chapter III - 1897-1919
Early Years at Tuskegee

In 1897, after joining the staff of Tuskegee Institute, two of George Washington Carver's former professors asked him to pen a brief sketch on his life. Carver replied:

> As nearly as I can trace my history I was about 2 weeks old when the war closed. My parents were both slaves. Father was killed shortly after my birth while hauling wood to town on an ox wagon. I had 3 sisters and one brother. Two sisters and my brother I know to be dead only as history tells me. Yet I do not doubt it as they are buried in the family burying ground.
>
> My sister, mother and myself were ku klucked, and sold in Arkansas and there are now so many conflicting reports concerning them I dare not say if they are dead or alive. Mr. Carver the gentlemen who owned my mother sent a man for us, but only I was brought back, nearly dead with whooping cough with the report that mother & sister was dead, although some say they saw them afterwards going north with the soldiers.
>
> My home was near Neosho Newton Co. Missouri where I remained until I was about 9 years old. My body was very feeble and it was a constant warfare between life and death to see who would gain the mastery——
>
> From a child I had an inordinate desire for knowledge, and especially music, painting, flowers, and the sciences, Algebra being one of my favorite studies.
>
> Day after day I spent in the woods alone in

order to collect my floral beauties and put them in my little garden I had hidden in brush not far from the house, as it was considered foolishness in that neighborhood to waste time on flowers.

And many are the tears I have shed because I would break the roots or flowers off some of my pets while removing them from the ground, and strange to say all sorts of vegetation succeeded to thrive under my touch until I was styled the plant doctor, and plants from all over the county would be brought to me for treatment. At this time I had never heard of botany and could scarcely read.

Rocks had an equal fascination for me and many are the basketful that I have been compelled to remove from the outside chimney corner of that old log house, with the injunction to throw them down hill. I obeyed but picked up the choicest ones and hid them in another place, and some how that same chimney corner would, in a few days or weeks be running over again to suffer the same fate. I have some of the specimens in my collection now and consider them the choicest of the lot. Mr. and Mrs. Carver were very kind to me and I thank them so much for my home training.

George Washington Carver National Monument, Diamond Grove, Missouri

They encouraged me to secure knowledge, helping me all they could, but this was quite limited. As we lived in the country, no colored schools were available so I was permitted to go 8 miles to a school at town (Neosho). This simply sharpened my appetite for more knowledge. I managed to secure all my meager wardrobe from my home and when they heard from me I was cooking for a wealthy family in Ft Scott Kans. for my board, cloths and school privileges.

Of course they were indignant and sent for me to come home at once, to die, as the family doctor had told them I would never live to see 21 years of age. I trusted God and pressed on (I had been a Christian since about 8 years old.) Sunshine and shadow were profusely intermingled, such as naturally befall a defenseless orphan by those who wish to prey upon them.

My health began improving and I remained here for two years. From here to Oletha Kans. to school. From there to Paola Normal School, from there to Minneapolis Kans. where I remained in school about 7 years finishing the high school, and in addition some Latin and Greek. From here to Kans. City entered a business college of short hand and typewriting. I was here to have a position in the Union telegraph Office as stenographer & typewriter, but the thirst for knowledge gained the mastery and I sought to enter Highland College at Highland Kans., but was refused on account of my color.

I went from here to Western part of Kans. where I saw the subject of my famous Yucca & cactus painting that went to the Worlds Fair. I drifted from here to Winterset Iowa, began as head cook in a large hotel. Many thanks here for the acquaintance of Mr. and Mrs. Dr. Milholland, who insisted upon me going to an Art School, and choose Simpson College for me.

The opening of school found me at Simpson attempting to run a laundry for my support and batching to economize. For quite one month I lived on prayer and beef suet and corn meal. Modesty prevented me telling my condition to strangers.

The news soon spread that I did laundry work and really needed it, so from that time on favors not only rained but poured upon me. I cannot speak too highly of the faculty, students and in fact the town generally. They all seemed to take pride in seeing if he or she might not do more for me than some one else.

But I wish to especially mention the names of Miss Etta M. Budd (my art teacher, Mrs. W.A. Liston & family, and Rev. A.D. Field & family. Aside from their substantial help at Simpson, were the means of my attendance at Ames. Please fix this to suit.)

I think you know my career at Ames and will fix it better than I. I will simply mention a few things. I received the prize offered for the best herbarium in cryptogamy. I would like to have said more about you Mrs. Liston and Miss Budd but feared you would not put it in about yourself, and I did not want one without all.

I received a letter from Mrs. Liston and she gave me an idea that it was not to be a book or anything of the kind this is only a fragmentary list. I knit, crochet, and made all my hose mittens etc. while I was in school. If this is not sufficient please let me know, and if it ever comes out in print I would like to see it.

God bless you all.

Geo. W. Carver [9]

On September 2, 1901, George W. Carver wrote from Tuskegee to his friends, John and Helen Milholland:

I think of you often and shall never forget what you were to my life, how much real help and inspiration you gave me. You, of course, will never know how much you done for a poor colored boy who was drifting here and there as a ship without a rudder. You helped to start me aright and what the Lord has in his kindness and wisdom permitted me to accomplish is due in a very great measure to your real genuine Christian spirits. How I wish the world was full of such people. What a different world it would be....

May God continue to bless and keep you.

Yours very gratefully,

Geo. W. Carver [10]

On November 28, 1902, George W. Carver wrote to the President of Tuskegee Institute, Booker T. Washington, regarding an unfortunate incident that resulted from the appearance of a white photographer, Miss Frances B. Johnston, who was traveling the south with a black teacher, Nelson E. Henry, to gather information on black schools:

Dear Mr. Washington,

I have just returned from a trip to Ramer, Alabama, where Mr. Henry is located, and I feel that you ought to know the exact condition there as it is the most distressing of any that I have ever seen in any place. In fact, I had the most frightful experience of my life there and for one day and night it was a very serious question indeed as to whether I would return to Tuskegee alive or not as the people were thoroughly bent upon bloodshed.

In all probability they have broken up the school. Mr. Henry was obliged to leave Ramer between the suns and the other teacher became so frightened that she left also.

The occasion of the disturbance was Miss Johnston, who went down on the same train that carried me down. The white people evidently knew that she was coming. The train was late in getting there but a number of people had gathered at the station to see what would happen.

I took Miss Johnston's valise and put it in the buggy for her. Mr. Henry drove her to his house and put out her valise and started to the hotel, then he was met by parties and after a few words was shot at three times.

Of course, he ran and got out of the way and Miss Johnston came to the house where I was. I got out at once and succeeded in getting her to the next station where she took the train the next morning.

The next day everything was in a state of turbulency and a mob had been formed to locate Mr. Henry and deal with him. They did not pay a great deal of attention to me as I kept out of the way as much as possible, but it was one of the worst situations that I have ever been it.

As things are now, the school is broken up and there seems to be no way of settling the difficulty. They say that what they want is to get hold of Mr. Henry and beat him nearly to death. I spoke to the people on Wednesday and they were-of course-very much disturbed.

I quieted them down as much as I could - which was very little. I had to walk nearly all night Tuesday night to keep out of their reach. Wednesday night I stayed four miles from the place and took the train six miles from Ramer next morning.

On Wednesday the place was patrolled by a white man walking up and down in front of the school house armed with a shot gun. I went down on Wednesday morning to see just what the situation was and I saw twelve horses saddled and tied to the fence of one of the chief promoters.

He saw me coming down the railroad and at once mounted his horse and came down to meet me. I stopped aside to examine some plants - just to see what he would do - and he came up and eyed me closely and spoke rather politely. He evidently thought I was Mr. Henry.

One of the gentlemen went down town that night to see what was being done and found that a mob was being made up for the night to take Mr. Henry. I succeeded in getting word to Mr. Henry to flee for his life, which he did. He is now in Montgomery.

Mr. Henry gone, they then telephoned over to the next station to see if Miss Johnston took the train the next morning. They wanted to know who took her to the train, and everything in detail.

A telegram was handed to a gentleman, which was evidently a fake - at least appeared so. If was purported to have come for Mr. Henry to induce him to come to the station. It was simply to find out where he was. I have never seen people so enraged.

Mr. Henry was doing a great work there and it grieves me to know that he must give it up. Miss Johnston was thoroughly grieved. I might say that she is the pluckiest woman I ever saw. She was not afraid for herself but shed bitter tears for Mr. Henry and for the school which is in all probability broken up.

They were preparing to have a splendid exhibition. In fact, the material was there and promised to be one of the best exhibitions that I have had the privilege of attending. The exhibits were large and fine and the people seemed very much encouraged.

Now as to the outcome, it is impossible to say. It stands just as I have related it to you. Mrs. Washington and I have talked the matter over here and we think it wise to say just as little as possible about it here. The people seem to be intensely bitter against any one who comes from Tuskegee.

Trusting you are quite well and that you had a pleasant Thanksgiving, I beg to remain,

Yours most sincerely,

G.W. Carver [11]

On May 28, 1907, George W. Carver wrote to Booker T. Washington regarding a Bible class he had begun at Tuskegee:

For your information only.

Mr. B.T. Washington,

About three months ago 6 or 7 persons met in my office one evening and organized a Bible class, and asked me to teach it. I consented to start them off. Their idea was to put in the 20 or 25 minutes on Sunday evenings which intervene between supper and chapel service.

We began at the first of the Bible and attempted to explain the Creation story in the light of natural and revealed religion and geological truths. Maps, charts plants and geological specimens were used to illustrate the work.

We have had an ave. attendance of 80 and often as high as 114. Thought these facts would help you in speaking of the religious life of the school. Very truly.

G.W. Carver [12]

On December 23, 1914, George W. Carver wrote to John and Helen Milholland, reporting on a car accident he was in and commented on the World War that was raging in Europe:

My dear friends,

I am glad to know that all are well, and am especially thankful that the good Lord has spared me to write to you. This summer I came near loosing my life, and I am yet unable to see how I could pass through such an ordeal and yet live. A large auto truck turned with several of us in it. One man was badly mashed up so much that he is yet after 7 months unable to walk. I was pinned down under the truck, badly bruised and cut up but no bones broken.

Every time I pick up a paper, I think of what General Sherman said war was. Words fail to describe the horror and suffering. It is making it very hard here for us. Not much money is coming in and how we will get along God only knows.

I have just learned that 25 girls are nearly barefooted and have not sufficient clothes to keep them decent or warm. Many boys are almost as bad, so we are going to do what we can for them...

Sincerely your friend,

Geo. W. Carver [13]

Chapter IV - 1920-1921
Y.M.C.A. & U.S. Congress

In the summer of 1920, the Young Men's Christian Association of Blue Ridge, North Carolina, invited Professor Carver to speak at their summer school for the southern states. Dr. Willis D. Weatherford, President of Blue Ridge, introduced him as the speaker. With his high voice surprising the audience, Professor Carver exclaimed humorously:

> I always look forward to introductions as opportunities to learn something about myself....

He continued:

> Years ago I went into my laboratory and said, "Dear Mr. Creator, please tell me what the universe was made for?"
>
> The Great Creator answered, "You want to know too much for that little mind of yours. Ask for something more your size, little man."
>
> Then I asked. "Please, Mr. Creator, tell me what man was made for."
>
> Again the Great Creator replied, "You are still asking too much. Cut down on the extent and improve the intent."
>
> So then I asked, "Please, Mr. Creator, will you tell me why the peanut was made?"
>
> "That's better, but even then it's infinite. What do you want to know about the peanut?"
>
> "Mr. Creator, can I make milk out of the peanut?"
>
> "What kind of milk do you want? Good Jersey milk or just plain boarding house milk?"

"Good Jersey milk."

And then the Great Creator taught me to take
the peanut apart and put it together again. And out of the
process have come forth all these products! [14]

Among the numerous products displayed was a bottle of *good
Jersey milk.* (Three-and-a-half ounces of peanuts produced one pint of
rich milk or one quart of boardinghouse blue john!) [15]

On January 21, 1921, at the request of the United Peanut Growers
Association, George Washington Carver addressed the U.S. House Ways
and Means Committee in Washington, D.C., regarding a proposed tariff
on imported peanuts. George expounded on the many potential uses of
the peanut as a means to improve the economy of the South. Initially
given only ten minutes to speak, the committee became so enthralled that
the Chairman said, "Go ahead Brother. Your time is unlimited!"

George spoke for one hour and forty-five minutes, explaining the
many foods products derived from the peanut:

If you go to the first chapter of Genesis, we can
interpret very clearly, I think, what God intended when
he said "Behold, I have given you every herb that bears
seed. To you it shall be meat." This is what He means
about it. It shall be meat. There is everything there to
strengthen and nourish and keep the body alive and
healthy. [16]

At the end of his address, the Committee Chairman asked:

"Dr. Carver, how did you learn all of these
things?"
Carver answered:
"From an old book"
"What book?" asked the Chairman.
Carver replied, "The Bible."
The Chairman inquired, "Does the Bible tell
about peanuts?"
"No, Sir" Dr. Carver replied, "But it tells about
the God who made the peanut. I asked Him to show me
what to do with the peanut, and He did."[17]

Chapter V - 1921-1922
Letters to a Professor,
a Student & Friends

On June 11, 1921, George W. Carver wrote to his old professor from Iowa State College, Dr. Louis H. Pammel, who had visited him at Tuskegee:

> Everyone wanted to hear you speak. I really wanted you to see the suit of clothes, hat, gloves, underwear, you helped fool me down town and bought for me, preparatory to going to Cedar Rapids to the Art exhibit with some of my pictures....
> Of course my microscope is just as good as new. I was glad to see that God had dealt so kindly with you, by giving you increased bodily vigor, great mental attainments, etc.
> When you were going out of your way to help a poor insignificant black boy, you were giving many "cups of cold water" in His name. The memory of yourself, Mrs. Pammel and the children are more dear to me than words can express. They served as lamps unto my feet and lights along my pathway...
> Sincerely and gratefully yours,
> G.W. Carver [18]

On January 9, 1922, George W. Carver wrote a thank you note to one of his students, L. Robinson, who had given him a Christmas present:

> Mr. L. Robinson,
> I wish to express through you to each member of the Senior class my deep appreciation for the fountain pen you so kindly and thoughtfully gave

me Christmas.

This gift, like all the others, is characterized by simplicity and thoughtfulness, which I hope each member will make the slogan of their lives.

As your father, it is needless for me to keep saying, I hope, except for emphasis, that each one of my children will rise to the full height of your possibilities, which means the possession of these eight cardinal virtues which constitutes a lady or gentleman.

1st. Be clean both inside and outside.

2nd. Who neither looks up to the rich or down on the poor.

3rd. Who loses, if needs be, without squealing.

4th. Who wins without bragging.

5th. Who is always considerate of women, children and old people.

6th. Who is too brave to lie.

7th. Who is too generous to cheat.

8th. Who takes his share of the world and lets other people have theirs.

May God help you to carry out these eight cardinal virtues and peace and prosperity be yours through life.

Lovingly yours,

G.W. Carver [19]

Dr. Louis H. Pammel (1862-1931), friend of Carver, 1903

In 1922, Mrs. Helen Milholland asked George W. Carver to write an outline of his life, which he entitled A Brief Sketch of My Life:

I was born in Diamond Grove, Mo., about the close of the great Civil War, in a little one-roomed log shanty, on the home of Mr. Moses Carver, a German by birth and the owner of my mother, my father being the property of Mr. Grant, who owned the adjoining plantation. I am told that my father was killed while hauling wood with an oxen team. In some way he fell from the load, under the wagon, both wheels passing over him.

At the close of the war the Ku Klux Klan was at its height in that section of Missouri. My mother was stolen with myself, a wee babe in her arms. My brother James was grabbed and spirited away to the woods by Mr. Carver. He tried to get me, but could not. They carried my mother and myself down into Arkansas, and sold my mother. At that time I was nearly dead with the whooping cough that I had caught on the way. I was so very frail and sick that they thought of course that I would die within a few days. Mr. Carver immediately sent a very fine race horse and some money to purchase us back. The man (Bently by name) returned with the money and myself, having given the horse for me. The horse was valued at $300. Every effort was made to find my mother, but to no avail.

In the meantime my only two sisters died and were buried. My bother James and I grew up together, sharing each other's sorrows on the splendid farm owned by Mr. Carver. When just a mere tot in short dresses my very soul thirsted for an education. I literally lived in the woods. I wanted to know every strange stone, flower, insect, bird, or beast. No one could tell me.

My only book was an old Webster's Elementary Spelling Book. I would seek the answer here without satisfaction. I almost knew that book by heart. At the age of 19 years my brother left the old home for Fayetteville,

Arkansas. Shortly after, at the age of 10 years, I left for Neosho, a little town just 8 miles from our farm, where I could go to school. Mr. and Mrs. Carver were perfectly willing for us to go where we could be educated the same as white children. I remained here about two years, got an opportunity to go to Fort Scott, Kansas with a family. They drove through the country.

Every year I went to school, supporting myself by cooking and doing all kinds of house work in private families. At the age of nineteen years I went back to see my brother and Mr. and Mrs. Carver. I had not improved much in stature, as I rode on a half-fare ticket. The conductor thought I was rather small to be traveling alone. I spent the summer here, and returned to Minneapolis, Kansas, where I finished my high school work.

The sad news reached me here that James, my only brother, had died with small pox. Being conscious as never before that I was left alone, I trusted God and pushed ahead. In working for others I had learned the minutia of laundering. I had opened a laundry for myself; got all I could do.

After finishing high school here I made application to enter a certain College in Iowa. I was admitted, went but when the President saw I was colored he would not receive me. I had spent nearly all of my money, and had to open a laundry here. I was liberally patroned by the students. I remained here until spring and went to Winterset, Iowa, as first cook in a large hotel.

One evening I went to a white church, and set in the rear of the house. The next day a handsome man called for me at the hotel and said his wife wanted to see me. When I reached the splendid residence I was astonished to recognize her as the prima dona in the choir. I was most astonished when she told me that my fine voice had attracted her. I had to sing quite a number of pieces for her and agreed to come to her house at least once a week; and from that time till now Mr. and Mrs. Milholland have been my warmest and most helpful friends.

I cooked at this hotel for some time, then opened a laundry for myself. I ran this laundry for one year. This same Mr. and Mrs. Milholland encouraged me to go to college. It was her custom to have me come at the day and rehearse to her the doings of the day. She would invariably laugh after such a recital and say, "Whoever heard of any one person doing half so many things."

She encouraged me to sing and paint, for which arts I had passionate fondness. In one years time I had saved sufficient money to take me to Simpson College, at Indianola, Iowa where I took art, music and college work. I opened a laundry here for my support. After all my matriculation fees had been paid I had 10 c worth of corn meal, and the 5 c I spent for beef suet. I lived on these two things one whole week—it took that long for the people to learn that I wanted clothes to wash. After that week I had many friends and plenty of work.

I would never allow anyone to give me money, no difference how badly I needed it. I wanted literally to earn my living. I remained here for three years; then entered the Iowa State College, at Ames, Iowa, where I pursued my Agricultural work, taking two degrees, Bachelor and Master.

After finishing my Bachelor's degree I was elected a member of the faculty, and given charge of the greenhouse, bacteriological laboratory, and the laboratory work in systematic botany.

Mr. Washington said he needed a man of my training. I accepted and came to Tuskegee nearly 27 years ago, and have been here ever since.[20]

On May 5, 1922, George W. Carver wrote to Dr. Louis H. Pammel:

My dear Dr. Pammel,
    In response to your queries of recent date, I beg to reply as follows:

1st. Born at Diamond Grove, Mo., just as freedom was declared, in a little one roomed log shanty on my master, Moses Carver's farm.

2nd. My education was picked up here and there. Mr. and Mrs. Carver taught me to read, spell and write just a little. I went to Neosho, Mo., public school for about nine months, then to Fort Scott town school, for about the same length of time. From there, I went to Olathe, Kans., where I attended the town public school for about two years.

Leaving there, I went to Minneapolis, Kansas, where I nearly finished my high school work. From here, I went to Indianola, Iowa, to Simpson College, where I took the College work and specialized in art and music.

From here I went to Ames, Iowa, to take a course in Agriculture, persuaded to do so by my art teacher, Miss Etta M. Budd, to whom I am greatly indebted for whatever measure of success that has come to me.

Iowa State

Dr. Louis Pammel and Dr. Carver,1928

Miss Budd helped me in whatever way she could; often going far out of her way to encourage and see that I had such things as I needed. During my six years in College, her interest in me never waned.

3rd. I do not now recall the exact date.

4th. I did odd jobs of all kinds for a number of the professors such as cutting wood, making gardens, working in the fields, helping clean house, taking care of the green house and the chemical, botanical and bacteriological laboratories.

5th.   Came   to

Tuskegee Institute, and took charge of the Agricultural Department here; kept it about fifteen years, then was given charge of the Agricultural Research work. I have kept this work in connection with the Experiment Station ever since.

6th. I have no words to adequately express my impressions of dear old I.S.C. All I am and all I hope to be, I own in a very large measure to this blessed institution.

7th. "Beardshear," was one of the biggest and best hearted men I have ever known and it was so pleasant and uplifting to come in contact with him.

"Wilson," the name Hon. James Wilson is sacred to me. He was one of the finest teachers that it has ever been my privilege to listen to. He taught a Sunday School class in which every student would have enrolled, if they had been allowed.

The class grew so large that he conceived a very unique plan to divide it, so he graduated some twenty or twenty-five of us who had been with him the longest. I happened to be one of the ones graduated. We all left him sad and reluctantly. We gave him to understand, in no uncertain terms, that we did not like it at all and out of our love for him, we went, but in less than two months we were all back again.

Our displeasure grieved him very much and he said to me, many times that he would never try to divide his class again, no matter how large it got.

Being a colored boy, and the crowded condition of the school, made it rather embarrassing for some, and it made the question of a room rather puzzling. Prof. Wilson said, as soon as he heard it, "Send

Brown Bros.

Prof. James Wilson (1836-1920) taught Carver at Iowa State and became Secretary of Agriculture under Presidents W. McKinley, T. Roosevelt and W.H. Taft.

him to me, I have a room," and he gave me his office and was very happy in doing so.

"Budd" was the father of Miss Etta M. Budd, heretofore mentioned, and my professor of Horticulture and a man much on the order of Prof. Wilson; kind, considerate, loving and loveable; a great teacher, and he made of his students his personal friends. Everybody loved Prof. Budd....

Miss Roberts was a teacher of rare ability. Her chief delight seemed to be that of helping the backward student. And many, many are the men and women today who rise up and call her blessed, for the help she gave them in more ways than one. I take especial delight in registering as one of that number....

Prof. H. Wallace is now Hon. Secretary of Agriculture, Washington, D.C. The heights to which he has risen testifies more strongly than any words of mine can. No one missed Prof. Wallace's class, if they could help it. He was a born teacher, a man too big in heart, mind and soul to be little in any particular. He, like all of my teachers, will never know how much he enthused and inspired me, as a student. [21]

Professor Joseph Lancaster Budd, who taught George Carver horticulture, pictured with his wife, Sarah Breed Budd, and their children, Etta May and Allen Joseph

On September 3, 1922, George
Carver wrote to Mrs. Helen Milholland:

Iowa State

My dear Mrs. Milholland,
How glad I was to get your card.... I
wonder if you have seen the little
book entitled Handicapped Winners
written by Miss Sara Estelle Haskin,
Educational Secy. of the Board of
Missions, Woman's work, M.E.
South. It is written for their Schools,
with the hope that it will bring about
a better feeling for the negro. It was
published by their publishing
house.... It has the "Peanut Wizard"
in it. Your name appears in it also...

*Prof. Henry C. Wallace (1836-
1930) taught Carver at Iowa
State and became U.S.
Secretary of Agriculture under
President Warren G. Harding.*

God is blessing me more and
more every day it seems. I hardly think you would know
me now I am quite gray, but pretty active yet.
Sincerely and gratefully yours,
Geo. W. Carver [22]

On September 17, 1922, George W. Carver wrote again to Mrs.
Helen Milholland, complimenting the draft of a biography she was
publishing on him:

My dear Mrs. Milholland,
How glad I was to get your good letter it seems
so refreshing to hear from you....
No, the book does not even approach yours and
I believe God in some way will provide a way for yours
to come out, I am anxious for you to see this little book
because it is to be put into their schools, for the
information of the white boys and girls down here who
seem to know so little about many types of colored
people....
Sincerely yours,
Geo. W. Carver [23]

Photograph courtesy of the Simpson College Archives, Indianola, IA

Dr. Carver with products from the peanut

Chapter VI - 1923-1924
Touching Young People's Lives

George Washington Carver developed a lifelong friendship with Mr. James T. Hardwick from the Virginia Polytechnic Institute. James' brother, Harry Hardwick, was the head football coach of the U.S. Naval Academy. In 1923, George Washington Carver commented to Mr. Hardwick:

> In my work I meet many young people who are seeking truth. God has given me some knowledge. When they let me, I try to pass it on to my boys. [24]

A close friend of George Carver from Iowa State College was Professor Henry C. Wallace, who later became President Warren G. Harding's Secretary of Agriculture.

His son, Henry A. Wallace, later studied under Carver at Iowa State, going on numerous nature hikes. Henry A. Wallace succeeded his father as U.S. Secretary of Agriculture and later served as Vice-President under Franklin D. Roosevelt. He described Carver as the "kindliest, most patient teacher I ever knew." [25]

Iowa State

Henry A. Wallace (1888-1965) was Carver's student at Iowa State, 1909. He later became U.S. Secretary of Agriculture and Vice President under Franklin D. Roosevelt.

On January 6, 1924, George W. Carver wrote to his former Professor, U.S. Secretary of Agriculture Henry C. Wallace:

I had been thinking of you more than usual here of late and "How God" had called you to perform the great service to humanity that you are now rendering.

I pray that He may continue to give you the guiding light that has attended your administration up to date in such a pronounced way.

Of course I never can repay you for being so kind, and indulgent to a poor little wayward black boy when in school. I wish that God in some way would show you how I appreciate it, and reward you accordingly....

Geo. W. Carver [26]

On May 21, 1924, George W. Carver wrote to Mr. James T. Hardwick:

My very dear friend, Mr. Hardwick,

My friend, God has indeed been good to me and is yet opening up wonders and allowing me to peep in as it were. I do love the things God has created, both animate and inanimate. As He speaks aloud through both, God willing, at Blue Ridge we will let Him talk to some of us.

You do me too much credit. I am not so good. I am just trying through Christ, to be a better man each day. Your spirit helps me so much. It is what my very soul has thirsted for all these years, a spirit that God likewise was developing to perform a great service to humanity, such as he is developing in you....

My "horoscope" tells me that God is yet going to do some thing for you that will astonish you.....Sincerely yours,

Geo. W. Carver [27]

On July 10, 1924, George W. Carver wrote to Mr. James T. Hardwick of Virginia:

Fri. morning. Dear Friend, I feel your loving spirit more than ever this morning. Thank God I feel the growth of the spirit within you.

My Beloved Friend, Mr. Hardwick:

What a joy always comes to me when I recognized your handwriting in the mail. I always say "bless his heart" meaning a letter from my beloved friend who is more dear to me than any words can express.

I love you and shall continue to do so for the Christ that is in you, both expressed and unexpressed. I love you also because Christ loves you and longs for you to come into the fullness of his glory.

Your words, my friend, are too strong. There is no danger of your being a hypocrite. You are struggling. You have not lost sight of self yet, but Thank God, you will.

As soon as you begin to read the great and loving God out of all forms of existence He has created, both animate and inanimate, then you will be able to Converse with Him, anywhere, everywhere, and at all times. Oh, what a fullness of joy will come to you. My dear friend, get the significance. God is speaking. "Look unto the hills from whence cometh thy help. Yes, go to the mountains if God so wills it."

Get ready to come down here for a week or so, should God ask you to do so. Somehow God seems to say to me that this may be so.

For months this vision from times to time comes to me. I think God wants you to begin reading Nature of your own accord first, then when you come here you will learn to interpret it with great rapidity. It may not be here. I may be thrown with you somewhere. Whatever the method is you must learn. Let us pray for guidance.

I have had eight letters from the boys already. Have heard from everyone in the cottage where I stayed. Two of them are coming down soon, they say.

Two have sent their pictures and others are coming. You and those other boys are all wrong. It is not me. I love you because I love Christ in you and whenever you reveal it I cannot help but love it. I loved those boys because Christ was there. As for you, my friend, you belong to me. You are mine. God gave you to me last year. I picked you out of the audience.

George Washington Carver (right) instructing student at Tuskegee Institute, 1902

If I remember correctly while speaking, those great spiritual windows (the eyes) of yours seemed to say, this is the person whom I have chosen to be a great help to you. You need him and maybe you can be of a little service to him. From that very time until now I have loved you so dearly.

God cannot use you as He wishes until you come into the fullness of his Glory. Don't get alarmed, friend, when doubts creep in. That is Old Satan. Pray, pray, pray. Neither be cast down or afraid if perchance you seem to wander from the path. This is sure to come to you if you trust too much in self.

Yes, my friend, you are going to grow. Your letters are always such a comfort to me. Do not get away somewhere and fail to write me regularly. You are now a part of my life and I long for your letters. Well, we both prayed that God would bless the message He sent me to deliver. He really seemed to bless it. At some of the personal interviews the boys wept. I have held my head and wept many times when I read so many of the letters they have written to me.

I fall, my friend, so far short of yours and their rating. God has already told you to go to the Mountains and commune with Him. Why not carry it out without He gives you a new message.

Oh, my friend, I am praying that God will come in and rid you entirely of self so you can go out after souls right, or rather have souls to seek the Christ in you. This is my prayer for you always.

Geo. W. Carver [28]

Classroom at Tuskegee Institute

Chapter VII - 1924-1925
Divine Inspiration & Criticism

George Washington Carver named his laboratory *God's Little Workshop,* and credited Divine inspiration for giving him the ideas of how to perform experiments. Though he never took any scientific textbooks into his laboratory, he was diligent to study as many scientific books as possible.

On November 19, 1924, Dr. George Washington Carver spoke to over 500 people at the Women's Board of Domestic Missions in New York City's Marble Collegiate Church:

> God is going to reveal to us things He never revealed before if we put our hands in His. No books ever go into my laboratory. The thing I am to do and the way of doing it are revealed to me. I never have to grope for methods. The method is revealed to me the moment I am inspired to create something new. Without God to draw aside the curtain I would be helpless. [29]

Locking the door to his laboratory, Dr. Carver confided:

> Only alone can I draw close enough to God to discover His secrets. [30]

On November 24, 1924, George W. Carver wrote the editor of the New York Times, correcting an editorial they ran entitled "Men of Science Never Talk that Way," in which they attempted to discredit Carver, his race and Tuskegee Institute:

> My dear Sir,
> I have read with much interest your editorial

pertaining to myself in the issue of November 20th. I regret exceedingly that such a gross misunderstanding should arise as to what was meant by "Divine inspiration." Inspiration is never at variance with information; in fact, the more information one has, the greater will be the inspiration.

Paul, the great Scholar, says, Second Timothy 2:15, "Study to show thyself approved unto God, a workman that needeth not to be ashamed, rightly dividing the word of truth."

Again he says in Galatians 1:12, "For I neither received it of man, neither was I taught it, but by the revelation of Jesus Christ."

Many, many other equally strong passages could be cited, but these two are sufficient to form a base around which to cluster my remarks. In the first verse, I have followed and am yet following the first word of study.

I am a graduate of the Iowa State College of Agriculture and Mechanical Arts, located at Ames, Iowa, taking two degrees in Scientific Agriculture. Did considerable work in Simpson College, Indianola, along the lines of Art, Literature and Music.

In Chemistry, the following persons have been inspiration and guide for study: Justin Von Liebig, Dr. Leroy J. Blinn, Dr. Ira Ramsen, Drs. L.L De Moninck, E. Dietz, Robert Mallet, William G. Valentin, J. Meritt Matthews, Edwin E. Slosson, M. Luckiesh, Harrison B. Howe, Charles Whiting Baker, Helen Abbott, Michael, Mad. Currie, Geo. J. Brush, Charles F. Chandler, G. Dragendorff, Frederick Hoffman, Josef Benson, Arthur C. Wright, M.W. O'Brine, Lucien Geschwind, Stillman, Wiley, Dana, Richards & Woodman, Harry Snyder, Coleman and Addyman, Meade Ostwald, Warrington, Winslow, and a number of others, all of which are in my own library with but a few exceptions.

In Botany, Loudon, Wood, Coulter, Stevens, Knight, Bailey, De Candole, Pammel, Bessey, Chapman, Gray, Goodale, Youkmans, Myers, Britton and Brown, Small, and others. These books are also in my library:

Dietaries, Henry, Richards, Mrs. Potter Palmer, Miles, Wing, Fletcher Berry, Kellogg, Nilson, and others.

In addition to the above, I receive the leading scientific publications. I thoroughly understand that there are scientists to whom the world is merely the result of chemical forces or material electrons. I do not belong to this class. I fully agree with the Rt. Rev. Irving Peake Johnson, D.D., bishop of Colorado in a little pamphlet entitled "Religion and the Supernatural." It is published and distributed by the Trinity Parish of your own city. I defy any one who has an open mind to read this leaflet through and then deny there is such a thing as Divine inspiration.

In evolving new creations, I am wondering of what value a book would be to the creator if he is not a master of analytical work, both qualitative and quantitative. I can see readily his need for the book from which to get his analytical methods. The master analyst needs no book; he is at liberty to take apart and put together substances, compatible or noncompatible to suit his own particular taste or fancy.

While in your beautiful city, I was struck with the large number of Taros and Yautias displayed in many of your markets; they are edible roots imported to this country largely from Trinidad, Puerto Rico, China, Dutch Guina and Peru. Just as soon as I saw these luscious roots, I marveled at the wonderful possibilities for their expansion. Dozens of things came to me while standing there looking at them. I would follow the same or similar lines I have pursued in developing products from the white potato. I know of no one who has ever worked with these roots in this way. I know of no book from which I can get this information, yet I will have no trouble in doing it.

If this is not inspiration and information from a source greater than myself, or greater than any one has wrought up to the present time, kindly tell me what it is.

"And ye shall know the truth and the truth shall make you free." John 8:32. Science is simply the truth

about anything.
Yours very truly,
Geo. W. Carver [31]

On January 15, 1925, George wrote to the Rev. Lyman Ward, founder of an industrial school in Camp Hill, Alabama:

My dear Bro. Ward,

Many, many thanks for your letter of Jan. 4th. How it lifted up my very soul, and made me to feel that after all God moves in a mysterious way His wonders to perform. I did indeed feel very badly for a while, not that the cynical criticism was directed at me, but rather at the religion of Jesus Christ. Dear Bro. I know that my Redeemer liveth.

I believe through the providence of the Almighty it was a good thing. Since the criticism was made I have had dozens of books, papers, periodicals, magazines, personal letters from individuals in all walks of life. Copies of letters to the editor of the Times are bearing me out in my assertion.

One of the prettiest little books comes from Ex. Govt. Osborne of Mich. His thesis on Divine Concord and so many, many dear letters like yours. I cannot think of filling 1/5 of the applications that are coming in for talks.

You may be interested to know that the greater part of my work now is among white colleges. I leave this week for N.C. where I will speak at the state univ. state college and two or three other colleges. Pray for me please that every thing said and done will be to His glory. I am not interested in science or any thing else that leaves God out of it.

Most sincerely your,
Geo. W. Carver [32]

Chapter VIII - 1925-1927
Science & the Great Creator

On March 24, 1925, George W. Carver wrote to Robert Johnson, an employee of Chesley Enterprises of Ontario:

> My dear Brother Johnson,
> How very interesting your letter is. I quite agree with you if God did not prompt your letters, you could not write those that really touch the heart as those of yours do.
> Of course I can not write such soul-stirring letters as yours, but I will do the best I can. I am so glad you like my motto. I try to live in that way and the Lord has, and is yet, blessing me so abundantly. Nothing could be more beautiful than your motto Others. Living for others is really the Christ life after all. Oh, the satisfaction, happiness and joy one gets out of it.
> I am so interested in the way you manage your saving account. God does indeed arrange it so that it never is quite depleted, unless there is some great emergency, then some soon comes in.
> Brother Johnson, I expect to stick to the path, I have no notion of wavering, regardless of how some may sneer. I know that my redeemer lives. Thank God I love humanity; complexion doesn't interest me one single bit. I am not rich in this world's goods, but thank God, like yourself, I have enough to live comfortably.
> I have the assurance that God will take care of me. He blesses me with the ability to earn a living, and gives me wisdom and understanding enough to lay a little by from time to time for the

proverbial "rainy day."

No, I am not for sale. God has given me what He has in trust to make of it a contribution to the world far greater than money can for myself. Yes my friend, I think I understood you. My letter to you probably was not as clear as it should have been.

I believe that science (truth) if it will take what you have had revealed to you. Search and continue to search. I am sure they will find a world of truth in it.

Less than 150 miles from where I live is one of the unexplained wonders of the country in what is known as "Blue Spring." The pool is about fifty feet in diameter, nearly round. One way you look at it, the water is as blue as indigo. Another way it is as clear as crystal, and you can see down, down, down. In the center is a spot fully four feet in diameter that boils up just as if a huge fire was under it; the water is not hot, not even warmer than other rivers or branch water; in fact, it is a little cooler than the average water. Hundreds of people far and near have examined it.

Large sums of money have been offered to any one who would dive down and find out where the water comes from. Some have tried it so they say, and have gone down a hundred feet or more and had to stop because the water threw them back with its force. No one knows where the water comes from. No difference how much it rains or how dry it gets, this little pool of boiling water is not affected in the least.

Your scripture references, I believe, can well be applied to this case. What I meant was that on the ocean waters journey back to fresh water again, it loses its salt some where, and I believe, in fact, it looks feasible to me that this salt water might travel some distance from the ocean before depositing its salt. If the vein was tapped after the salt had been deposited, a salt mine of dry salt would be the result, if before it gave up its salt, a salt well would be the result.

It seems to me that you have opened a most interesting and valuable line of investigation ....

Most sincerely yours.
Geo. W. Carver [33]

On March 24, 1925, George W. Carver wrote to Rev. Kunzman of Seattle:

> My dear Rev. Kunzman,
> Thank you for your good letter....
> Now as to your question. I regret that I cannot be of much service to you as I have not devoted much time to such investigations in proportion to the almost life time researches of some.
> I am interested of course, intensely interested. My life time study of nature in it's many phases leads me to believe more strongly than ever in the Biblical account of man's creation as found in Gen. 1:27 "And God created man in his own image, in the image of God

Photograph courtesy of the Simpson College Archives, Indianola, IA

Dr. Carver in greenhouse

George Washington Carver in laboratory

created He him; male and female created he them."

Of course sciences through all of the ages have been searching for the so called "missing link" which enables us to interpret man from his very beginning, up to his present high state of civilization.

I am fearful lest our finite researches will be wholly unable to grasp the infinite details of creation, and therefore we lose the great truth of the creation of man.

Yours very truly,

Geo. W. Carver [34]

On March 1, 1927, George W. Carver wrote to Jack Boyd, a YMCA official in Denver, Colorado:

My beloved Friend, Mr. Boyd,

How good of you to write me, and such a wonderful letter it is....

One of the most beautiful, hopeful, and encouraging things of growing interest, is that there is springing up here and there groups of college bred young men and women, who are willing to know us by permitting themselves to get acquainted with us.

The two little snaps are so beautiful, naturally, God has been so lavish in the display of His handiwork. It is indeed so much more impressive however, when you feel that God met with that fine body of students.

My dear friend, I am so glad that God is using you in such an effective way.

My beloved friend, I do not feel capable of

writing a single word of counsel to those dear young people, more than to say that my heart goes out to every one of them, regardless of the fact that I have never seen them and may never do so.

I want them to find Jesus, and make Him a daily, hourly, and momently part of themselves.

O how I want them to get the fullest measure of happiness and success out of life. I want them to see the Great Creator in the smallest and apparently the most insignificant things about them.

How I long for each one to walk and talk with the Great Creator through the things he has created.

How I thank God every day that I can walk and talk with Him. Just last week I was reminded of His omnipotence, majesty and power through a little specimen of mineral sent me for analysis, from Bakersfield, California. I have dissolved it, purified it, made conditions favorable for the formation of crystals, when lo before my very eyes, a beautiful bunch of sea green crystals have formed and alongside of them a bunch of snow white ones.

Marvel of marvels, how I wish I had you in God's little work-shop for a while, how your soul would be thrilled and lifted up.

My beloved friend, keep your hand in that of the Master, walk daily by His side, so that you may lead others into the realms of true happiness, where a religion of hate, (which poisons both body and soul) will be unknown, having in its place the "Golden Rule" way, which is the "Jesus Way" of life, will reign supreme.

Then, we can walk and talk with Jesus momentarily, because we will be attuned to His will and wishes, thus making the Creation story of the world non-debatable as to its reality.

God, my beloved friend is infinite the highest embodiment of love. We are finite, surrounded and often filled with hate. We can only understand the infinite as we loose the finite and take on the infinite.

My dear friend, my friendship to you cannot

*George Washington Carver
performing research in his laboratory*

possibly mean what yours does to me. I talk to God through you, you help me to see God through another angle....

   Most sincerely yours,

   G.W. Carver [35]

On December 13, 1927, George W. Carver wrote to the Hon. Leon McCord, circuit court judge of the Fifteenth Judicial District, Montgomery, Alabama:

> My esteemed friend Judge McCord,
>
> Yours received yesterday evening.
>
> There are times when one's powers of expression fail to convey the meaning of the heart. I find myself at this moment utterly far adrift upon the high seas without either compass or rudder, as far as the satisfactory power of expression is concerned.
>
> I read and reread your wonderful letter over several times. I reveled in its sublimity of thought and rare literary gift of expression to which the Great Creator has bequeathed to but few men.
>
> There are two things which puzzle me greatly. First, that a person as busy as you must needs be would take the time to write such a letter. Second, and the most puzzling of all is that you are talking about me, a subject so unworthy of such sublimity of thought and expression.
>
> As I sat in my little "den" reading and pondering over it, nature came to my relief when I was attracted by a strangely mellow light falling upon the paper. I looked up and out of the window toward the setting sun, which was just disappearing behind the horizon leaving a halo of never to be forgotten glory and beauty behind it. It seems as if I have never been conscious of such beauty and sublimity. The variety, brilliancy of color and arrangement were awe inspiring. As I sat there unconscious of everything except the scene before me, behold, before my very eyes it changed from the marvelous rainbow colors to the soft, ethereal "Rembrantian" browns and the midnight blues of

Maxfield Parrish. But the most marvelous of all was the pristine light which came from behind those strangely beautiful clouds; the light was like unto bright silver dazzling in its brightness, and weird in the manner of its diffusion.

As I came to myself I said aloud, O God, I thank Thee for such a direct manifestation of Thy goodness, majesty and power.

I thought of how typical this scene which had just passed into never to be forgotten history was of my good friend judge Leon McCord, whom I have known for more than a quarter of a century, a person occupying a most responsible and trying position, a position which makes most men cold, severe, unsympathetic, and sometimes cruel, but with my friend, the Judge, many, many thousands will rise up and call him blessed because you have been and are yet ever on the alert to help humanity.

Your "Big Brothers' Bible Class" is one of the strongest testimonials of the above statement.

In this fast approaching season of special reminders of "Peace on earth good will to men", may He who has kept, guided and prospered you during all of these years bring to you and yours additional joys and successes.

Yours with much love and admiration,
G.W. Carver [36]

Iowa State

George Washington Carver at Tuskegee Institute

George Washington Carver in his laboratory

George Washington Carver - His Life & Faith in His Own Words

Chapter IX - 1928-1930
Out of Doors, Home Folks & Truth

During one of Jim Hardwick's visits to Tuskegee Institute in 1928, he asked Dr. Carver to share some of his observations about God. Dr. Carver responded:

As a very small boy exploring the almost virgin woods of the old Carver place, I had the impression someone had just been there ahead of me. Things were so orderly, so clean, so harmoniously beautiful. A few years later in this same woods I was to understand the meaning of this boyish impression. Because I was practically overwhelmed with the sense of some Great Presence. Not only had someone been there. Someone was there....

Years later when I read in the Scriptures, "In Him we live and move and have our being," I knew what the writer meant. Never since have I been without this consciousness of the Creator speaking to me....

The out of doors has been to me more and more a great cathedral in which God could be continuously spoken to and heard from....

Man, who needed a purpose, a mission, to keep him alive, had one. He could be...God's co-worker.... My attitude toward life was also my attitude toward science. Jesus said one must be born again, must become as a little child. He must let no laziness, no fear, no stubbornness keep him from his duty.

If he were born again he would see life from such a plane he would have the energy not to be impeded in his duty by these various sidetrackers and inhibitions. My work, my life, must be in the spirit of a little child seeking only to know the truth and follow it.

My purpose alone must be God's purpose - to increase the welfare and happiness of His people. Nature will not permit a vacuum. It will be filled with something. Human need is really a great spiritual vacuum which God seeks to fill....

With one hand in the hand of a fellow man in need and the other in the hand of Christ, He could get across the vacuum and I became an agent. Then the passage, "I can do all things through Christ which strengtheneth me," came to have real meaning.

As I worked on projects which fulfilled a real human need forces were working through me which amazed me. I would often go to sleep with an apparently insoluble problem. When I woke the answer was there.

Why, then, should we who believe in Christ be so surprised at what God can do with a willing man in a laboratory? Some things must be baffling to the critic who has never been born again.

By nature I am a conserver. I have found nature to be a conserver. Nothing is wasted or permanently lost in nature. Things change their form, but they do not cease to exist.

After I leave this world I do not believe I am through. God would be a bigger fool than even a man if he did not conserve what seems to be the most important thing he has yet done in the universe. This kind of reasoning may aid the young.

When you get your grip on the last rung of the ladder and look over the wall as I am now doing you don't need their proofs. You see. You know you will not die. [37]

On January 25, 1929, George W. Carver wrote to Mrs. Eva Goodwin in Neosho, Missouri. He referred to her family as "homefolks," as she was the daughter of one of Carver's boyhood playmates, Thomas Williams, who was a great-nephew of Moses Carver:

My dear Mrs. Goodwin,

It is impossible for you to know how your letter made me feel, if you had only been a hundred mile or so away I would have started immediately to see you.

I have sat and looked long and hard at your Father's picture. While he has changed quite as much as I have, I can still discern that handsome kindly face, which made him to me ideal.

Of course you are happy to do the things for him, how I love this picture, one of my dearest boyhood playmates.

If I go to Oklahoma, the way I went before I will pass through Neosho, and it may be that I can arrange to stop over a day, or between trains at least. And see your dear Father and the rest. I am too beginning to feel the weight of years and cannot do much traveling now.

How I would love to get with your Father and talk over old times at home, indeed you really are my home folks.

Thank you for the clipping referring to the death of dear Mr. Carver, (Uncle Mose) I treasure it very much.

How delightful to have you speak of your Father in that way. I believe every word of it, his face shows it.

Yes I can remember you as a little girl, used to hold you on my lap. I certainly would appreciate any pictures of the old homeplace. I am sure it has changed very much.

I thank the good people for their words of approval, why should I not be able to do pretty well, I certainly had good home training by my "home folks".

My heart indeed goes out to my dear "Home Folks", Love and the best of wishes to your good neighbors.

I am sincerely yours,
G.W. Carver [38]

*George Washington Carver
engaged in laboratory research.*

On February 24, 1930, George W. Carver wrote to Hubert W. Pelt of the Phelps Stokes Fund, in which he included a brief essay entitled "How to Search for Truth":

I believe the Great Creator of the universe had young people in mind when the following beautiful passages were written:

In the 12th chapter of Job and the 7th & 8th verses, we are urged thus: But ask now the beasts and they shall teach thee; and the fowls of the air, and they shall tell thee. Or speak to the earth, and it shall teach thee; and the fishes of the sea shall declare unto thee.

In St. John the 8th chapter and 32nd verse, we have this remarkable statement:

And ye shall know the truth and the truth shall make you free. Were I permitted to paraphrase it, I would put it thus: And you shall know science and science shall set you free, because science is truth.

There is nothing more assuring, more inspiring, or more literally true than the above passages from Holy Writ.

We get closer to God as we get more intimately and understandingly acquainted with the things he has created. I know of nothing more inspiring than that of making discoveries for ones self.

The study of nature is not only entertaining, but instructive and the only true method that leads up to the development of a creative mind and a clear understanding of the great natural principles which surround every branch of business in which we may engage. Aside from this it encourages investigation, stimulates and develops originality in a way that helps the student to find himself more quickly and accurately than any plan yet worked out. The singing birds, the buzzing bees, the opening flower, and the budding trees, along with other forms of animate and inanimate matter, all have their marvelous creation story to tell each searcher for truth....

The singing birds, the buzzing bees, the opening flower, and the budding trees, along with other forms of animate and inanimate matter, all have their marvelous creation story to tell each searcher for truth....

We doubt if there is a normal boy or girl in all Christendom endowed with the five senses who have not watched with increased interest and profit, the various forms, movements and the gorgeous paintings of the butterfly, many do not know, but will study with increased enthusiasm the striking analogy its life bears to the human soul.

Even the ancient Greeks with their imperfect knowledge of insects recognized this truth, when they gave the same Greek name psyche to the Soul, or the spirit of life, and alike to the butterfly.

They sculptured over the effigy of their dead the figure of a butterfly floating away as it were in his breath. Poets to this day follow the simile.

More and more as we come closer and closer in touch with nature and its teachings are we able to see the Divine and are therefore fitted to interpret correctly the various languages spoken by all forms of nature about us.

From the frail little mushroom, which seems to spring up in a night and perish ere the morning sun sinks to rest in the western horizon, to the giant red woods of the Pacific slope that have stood the storms for centuries and vie with the snow-capped peaks of the loftiest mountains, in their magnificence and grandeur.

First, to me, my dear young friends, nature in its varied forms are the little windows through which God permits me to commune with Him, and to see much of His glory, majesty, and power by simply lifting the curtain and looking in.

Second, I love to think of nature as unlimited broadcasting stations, through which God speaks to us every day, every hour and every moment of our lives, if we will only tune in and remain so.

Third, I am more and more convinced, as I search

for truth that no ardent student of nature, can "Behold the lilies of the field"; or "Look unto the hills", or study even the microscopic wonders of a stagnant pool of water, and honestly declare himself to be an Infidel.

To those who already love nature, I need only to say, pursue its truths with a new zest, and give to the world the value of the answers to the many questions you have asked the greatest of all teachers-Mother Nature.

To those who have as yet not learned the secret of true happiness, which is the joy of coming into the closest relationship with the Maker and Preserver of all things: begin now to study the little things in your own door yard, going from the known to the nearest related unknown for indeed each new truth brings one nearer to God.

With love and best wishes,
G.W. Carver [39]

George Washington Carver engaged in research in his laboratory.

Photograph courtesy of the Simpson College Archives, Indianola, IA

Dr. Carver in his laboratory at Tuskegee Institute

Chapter X - 1931-1933
Prayer & God's Direction

On July 24, 1931, George W. Carver wrote to Miss Isabelle Coleman of Greensboro, North Carolina:

> My dear Miss Coleman,
> Thank you very much for your splendid letter. I thoroughly believe you can get a much better subject to go in your book than myself. After thinking it over again, searching around, if you still feel that I ought to go in there, you have my permission.
> The facts in "Upward Climb" are correct, as the writer came here and got the story.
> As to being a Christian, please write to Mr. Hardwick, Y.M.C.A., 706, Standard Building, Atlanta, Georgia. The dear boy made a ten days tour with me through Virginia, North Carolina, and Tennessee, where I lectured to a number of colleges and universities. We came together in prayer often to get our spiritual strength renewed. Whenever we come into a great project, we meet and ask God's guidance. Mr. Hardwick will tell you things that I could not. We both believe in Divine guidance. Prov. 3:6; Phil. 4:13; Psalms 119:18; these are our slogan passages.
> I was just a mere boy when converted, hardly ten years old. There isn't much of a story to it. God just came into my heart one afternoon while I was alone in the "loft" of our big barn while I was shelling corn to carry to the mill to be ground into meal.
> A dear little white boy, one of our neighbors, about my age, came by one Saturday morning and in talking and playing he told me he was going to Sunday school tomorrow morning. I was eager to know what a

Sunday school was. He said they sang hymns and prayed. I asked him what prayer was and what they said. I do not remember what he said; only remember that as soon as he left I climbed up into the "loft", knelt down by the barrel of corn and prayed as best I could. I do not remember what I said. I only recall that I felt so good that I prayed several times before I quit.

My brother and myself were the only colored children in the neighborhood and of course, we could not go to a church or Sunday school, or school of any kind.

That was my simple conversion, and I have tried to keep the faith.

Games were very simple in my boyhood days in the country. Baseball, running, jumping, swimming, and checkers constituted the principle ones. I played all of them.

My favorite song was "Must Jesus Bear the Cross Alone and all the world go free, etc."

If I had leisure time from roaming the woods and fields, I put it in knitting, crocheting, and other forms of fancy work. I am sending you, under separate cover, some literature which may be of service.

Very sincerely yours,
G.W. Carver [40]

On March 1, 1932, George W. Carver wrote to Mr. Zissler:

My esteemed friend, Mr. Zissler,

Before beginning the various routine duties of the day, I feel that I can start the day off in no better way than to pray that all is going well with you, and wish you could share with me the supreme expression of The Great Creator as He speaks to me so vividly through my beautiful Amaryllis (allies) that are opening daily in my windows in the little den I call my room.

Ten of these great flowers are open now, one that measures 10 inches in diameter, some of them are striped, spotted and otherwise penciled as exquisitely as orchids. These are my own breeding and shows what man (in the generic) can do when he allows God to speak through him.

> May God ever bless and keep you.
> So sincerely yours,
> G.W. Carver [41]

On July 1, 1932, George W. Carver wrote to Mr. James T. Hardwick:

> My Beloved Spiritual Boy, Mr. Hardwick,
> I must tell you about an experience I had today, which shows so clearly that God moves in a mysterious way His wonders to perform.
> Before we left for Miss. while dear Howard was here the first time, I made some collections of fungi some distance away. Occasionally my mind would urge me to go back there again. The urge became so strong this morning that I went. I found the place grown up with weeds and briars.
> I began pulling the dead limbs out but the wasps had built a nest in it and soon ran me away without stinging me. I stood afar off quite perplexed, started home, proceeded a little ways and spied another pile of brush. I went to it and found it to be one of the richest finds that I had yet made.
> God closed the first door that I might see one open with greater opportunities. This is often so when we are sorely disappointed in some of our fondest dreams.
> You have seemed to be with me all day today. May God ever be with my great spiritual boy, my pioneer boy, my oldest boy, in fact God's pioneer boy.
> With so much love and admiration,
> G.W. Carver [42]

George Washington Carver engaged in botany research

George Washington Carver - His Life & Faith in His Own Words

Chapter XI - 1934-1936
Healing & Suffering Humanity

In the 1930s, before Dr. Jonas Salk developed a successful vaccine, the feared disease of polio killed thousands and left others with atrophied muscles and useless limbs. Dr. George W. Carver developed a massage therapy using peanut oil, to help the victims of polio and infantile paralysis regain the use of their limbs. The Associated Press carried an article on this in December of 1933. Though physicians later gave more credit to his innovative use of massage technique rather than the oil, Prof. Carver had many documented recoveries.

On December 16, 1934, George W. Carver wrote to the mother of James Hardwick:

> My esteemed friend Mrs. Hardwick,
> Thank you so much for your beautiful card with its Greetings. I have not written to you in a long time, but my thoughts and prayers have been for you daily.
> Our patients have usurped almost all of my spare time. God continues to speak through the oils in a truly marvelous way.
> I have patients who come to me on crutches, who are now walking 6 miles without tiring, without either crutch or cane. (one man).
> My last patient today was one of the sweetest little 5 year old boys, who 3 months ago they had to carry in my room, being paralyzed from the waist down. When I had finished the massage today, much to our astonishment he dressed himself and stood up and walked across the floor without any support. He is a handsome little fellow and so happy that he is improving, (and I

too).

I said Our patients, because I feel that your prayers help to make it possible.

Since last Dec. 31st I have received 2020 letters, plus the people who come every day and almost every night for treatment. It is truly marvelous what God is doing.

Continue to pray for me please that I may be a more fit medium through which He can Speak....

I am so gratefully yours,

G.W. Carver [43]

On March 15, 1935, George W. Carver wrote to the Rev. Thomas O. Parish of Topeka, Kansas:

My great Spiritual friend,

Your letter came as a great spiritual message to let me know that God was speaking to me through you. Truly God is speaking through these peanut oils that I am working with. Marvelous, some come to me on crutches, canes etc., and in time go away walking. One father brought his dear little afflicted boy 200 miles to me this morning. (Infantile paralysis).

How I do thank you for your prayers. A Ga. pastor of a large church over in Ga. has just informed me that the whole congregation prayed for me last night.

God moves in a mysterious way and is performing wonders. Keep praying for me please.

May God ever bless, keep, guide and prosper you.

Gratefully yours.

G.W. Carver [44]

On March 22, 1935, George W. Carver wrote to the mother of James T. Hardwick:

My esteemed friend, Mrs. Hardwick,

My but it seems so good to hear from you. A

person as busy as you must needs be does not have much time for writing. How wonderful that you could actually come to Tuskegee, I cannot yet describe my feelings for such a great treat.

I have not been able to make any long trips this fall or winter. I miss being with dear "Jimmie", so much, the precious boy is a real part of my life, but I can understand, why I hear from him so little now, he is on the road.

I hope I can get to the Retreat for one day at last, but I am not sure my strength will hold out. God is surely showing some of His Glory, majesty and power with some of my patients, they are improving so fast that one is forced to know that the day of miracles are not yet over....

Mrs. Hardwick, I neglected to say the these patients I am working on are our patients, God is answering the prayers of those who are praying for me....

Very sincerely yours,

G.W. Carver [45]

On September 30, 1935, George W. Carver wrote to the Rev. Thomas O. Parrish of Topeka, Kansas:

My esteemed friend, Rev. Parish,

Your splendid letter has been here for a long time. I have been trying to find a few moments that I could call mine in which to answer.

I have now before me 3,000 or more letters from suffering humanity, besides the people who come to see me every day and every night. I often have to refuse to see any one until I can get a little rest.

Your letters to me are great spiritual message. I appreciate your prayers much more than I have words to express. Ask your congregation to please remember me in their silent prayers that God may continue to manifest through me more of His glory, majesty, and power. I need to become a better medium through which He can speak.

I trust your congregation will learn early the true secret of success, happiness, and power, as embodied in the four passages in the order named:

1. Sec. Cor. 3:5&6
2. Sec. Tim. 2:15
3. Prov. 3:6,
4. Phil. 4:13

I am

Most sincerely and gratefully yours,

G.W. Carver [46]

George Washington Carver studying

Chapter XII - 1937-1943
Public Speaking & Wisdom on Life

On March 17, 1937, George W. Carver wrote to the editor of the Roanoke [Alabama] Leader, Mr. Stevenson, whose son he had treated for paralysis:

> My esteemed friend, Mr. Stevenson,
>
> Thank you so very much for your splendid letter...
>
> I attempted to give a little demonstration on the Creation Story as set forth in the Bible and geology. In other words, I attempted to show that there was no conflict between science and religion. I had a great many illustrations from my geological collection, showing many fossils which told their own story. I had quite a large audience, and they seemed to get a little out of it. It was something so distinctly new to them that they probably overrated its value....
>
> Very sincerely and gratefully yours,
>
> G.W. Carver [47]

On January 28, 1938, George W. Carver wrote to Harry O. Abbott, who served as his traveling secretary:

> I have just received a remarkable letter from Dr. Glen Clark of St. Paul, Minn., wanting me to come as his guest to St. Paul on April 5 or 6, all expenses paid, plus $100 honorarium, with definite

provisions made by the president of the L. and N.R.R. for drawing room and every other comfort that can be provided.

He said that they would have absolutely no trouble in filling an auditorium which holds 2100 people. The occasion is the meeting of a very spiritual group that is arranging a series of lectures on bringing Christ into our lives during the week before Easter....

Yours very sincerely,

G.W. Carver [48]

On August 24, 1940, George W. Carver wrote to a Tuskegee, Alabama, minister, Rev. Haygood:

My esteemed friend, Rev. Haygood,

Thank you very much for your fine letter....

You are quite right with reference to your interpretation about what I mean when I say to young people that I hope they will be bigger than the pulpit. That is really what I mean-that I want them to be bigger than the pulpit and get them to study the great Creator through the things he has created, as I feel that He talks to us through these things that he has created. I know, in my own case, that I get so much consolation a so much information in this way, and indeed the most significant sermons that it has ever been my privilege to learn has been embodied in just that.

I thank you, also, for your sermon at the Greenwood Baptist Church, and if we do not take Christ seriously in our every day life, all is a failure because it is an every day affair. If we can just understand that the Golden Rule way of living is the only correct method, and the only Christ like method, this will settle all of our difficulties that bother us....

Very sincerely and gratefully yours,

G.W. Carver [49]

On September 7, 1940, George W. Carver wrote to Mr. and Mrs. Woods, who had given him some dahlias:

My dear Mr. Woods,

This is just to extend to you and Mrs. Woods greetings and to let you know as best I can how much I appreciate the exquisite Dahlias that you brought me.

I remember as a boy a little expression that has lingered with me all through life. It said, "that flowers were the sweetest things that God ever made and forgot to put a soul into it." It was one of the things that impressed me so very much that I always remembered, but as I grow older and study plant life, I am convinced that God didn't forget to do anything that was worthwhile.

When we think of the origin of the Dahlia, how it started from a little flower not much larger than a ten cent piece, single only, I appreciate the fact that the great Creator who made man in the likeness of his image to be co-partner with him in creating some of the most beautiful and useful things in the world, and it developed his mind, I can really see why he did not put the soul into the flower. He put it into us, and we expressed it in the development of just such beautiful flowers as you have sent me, and I know that you both are stronger and better from growing these beautiful messengers from the Creator and the fact that you wanted to share them with me is a thought so beautiful that I have no language to express it.

They will last for days and the memory of them, and the spirit which prompted the growing, and the bringing of them to me will always remain.

I am

Sincerely and gratefully yours,

George W. Carver, Director [50]

On December 16, 1941, George W. Carver wrote to the Rev. Carl A. Blackman of Kansas City, Missouri:

> My dear Rev. Blackman,
> In answer to your rather difficult request I beg to say as follows: My prayers seem to be more of an attitude than anything else. I indulge in very little lip service, but ask the Great Creator silently daily, and often many times per day to permit me to speak to Him through the three great Kingdoms of the world, which He has created, viz.-the animal, mineral and vegetable Kingdoms; their relations to each other, to us, our relations to them and the Great God who made all of us. I ask Him daily and often momently to give me wisdom, understanding and bodily strength to do His will, hence I am asking and receiving all the time.
> Very sincerely yours,
> G.W. Carver [51]

George Washington Carver remarked:

> The secret of my success? It is simple. It is found in the Bible, "In all thy ways acknowledge Him and He shall direct thy paths."[52]

In 1939, George Washington Carver was awarded the Roosevelt Medal, with the declaration:

> To a scientist humbly seeking the guidance of God and a liberator to men of the white race as well as the black. [53]

Appendix

Booker Taliaferro Washington (April 5, 1856-November 14, 1915), was an outstanding African-American educator, writer and reformer. He was born a slave on a plantation in Franklin County, Virginia, and worked in the salt and coal mines of West Virginia. His desire for learning led him to attend school at night and, at age sixteen, leave home and walk nearly 500 miles to attend Hampton Institute, which was founded by former Union General Samuel Chapman Armstrong. Working his way through school, Booker T. Washington

Booker T. Washington

graduated in 1875. He taught at Malden, West Virginia, and later at the Hampton Institute. In 1881, he founded Tuskegee Institute in Alabama with only 30 students, and over the next thirty-three years oversaw its growth to over 2,000. He recruited George Washington Carver as a professor, and was friends with the leading men of his day, including Andrew Carnegie, William Howard Taft, and Calvin Coolidge. He addressed audiences around the world and wrote: *Up From Slavery,* 1901, and *The Future of the American Negro,* 1899. He was the first African American to have his picture on a U.S. postage stamp, 1940, the first African American elected to the Hall of Fame, 1945, and the first Black to have his image on a U.S. coin, 1946.

In his book, Up From Slavery, Booker T. Washington wrote:

> In the city of Boston I have rarely called upon an individual for funds that I have not been thanked for calling, usually before I could get an opportunity to thank the donor for the money. In that city the donors seem to feel, in a large degree, that an honour is being conferred upon them in their being permitted to give. Nowhere else have I met with, in so large a measure, this fine and Christlike spirit as in the city of Boston, although there are many notable instances of it outside

that city. I repeat my belief that the world is growing in the direction of giving....

In my efforts to get money [for Tuskegee Institute] I have often been surprised at the patience and deep interest of the ministers, who are besieged on every hand and at all hours of the day for help. If no other consideration had convinced me of the value of the Christian life, the Christlike work which the Church of all denominations in America has done during the last thirty-five years for the elevation of the black man would have made me a Christian. In a large degree it has been the pennies, the nickels, and the dimes which have come from the Sunday-schools, the Christian Endeavour societies, and the missionary societies, as well as from the church proper, that have helped to elevate the Negro at so rapid a rate....

The more I come into contact with wealthy people, the more I believe that they are growing in the direction of looking upon their money simply as an instrument which God has placed in their hand for doing good with. I never go to the office of Mr. John D. Rockefeller, who more than once has been generous to Tuskegee, without being reminded of this. The close, careful, and minute investigation that he always makes in order to be sure that every dollar that he gives will do the most good—an investigation that is just as searching as if he were investing money in a business enterprise—convinces me that the growth in this direction is most encouraging....

When speaking directly in the interests of the Tuskegee Institute, I usually arrange, some time in advance, a series of meetings in important centres. This takes me before churches, Sunday-schools, Christian Endeavour Societies, and men's and women's clubs. When doing this I sometimes speak before as many as four organizations in a single day....

Atlanta was literally packed, at the time, with people from all parts of the country, and with representatives of foreign governments, as well as with military and civic organizations. The afternoon papers had forecasts of the next day's proceedings in flaring headlines. All this tended to add to my burden. I did not sleep much that night. The next morning, before day, I went carefully over what I planned to say. I also kneeled down and asked God's blessing upon my effort. Right here, perhaps, I ought to add that I make it a rule never to go before an audience, on any occasion, without asking the blessing of God upon what I want to say....

While a great deal of stress is laid upon the industrial side of the work at Tuskegee, we do not neglect or overlook in any degree the religious and spiritual side. The school is strictly undenominational, but it is thoroughly Christian, and the spiritual training or the students is not neglected. Our preaching service, prayer-meetings, Sunday-school, Christian Endeavour Society, Young Men's Christian Association, and various missionary organizations, testify to this....

In the school we made a special effort to teach our students the meaning of Christmas, and to give them lessons in its proper observance. In this we have been successful to a degree that makes me feel safe in saying that the season now has a new meaning, not only through all that immediate region, but, in a measure, wherever our graduates have gone....

While the institution is in no sense denominational, we have a department known as the Phelps Hall Bible Training School, in which a number of students are prepared for the ministry and other forms of Christian work, especially work in the country districts. What is equally important, each one of the students works . . . each day at some industry, in order to get skill and the love of work, so that when he goes out from the institution he is prepared to set the people with whom he goes to labour a proper example in the matter of industry....

It is now long ago that I learned this lesson from General Samuel Chapman Armstrong, and resolved that I would permit no man, no matter what his colour might be, to narrow and degrade my soul by making me hate him. With God's help, I believe that I have completely rid myself of any ill feeling toward the Southern white man for any wrong that he may have inflicted upon my race. I am made to feel just as happy now when I am rendering service to Southern white men as when the service is rendered to a member of my own race. I pity from the bottom of my heart any individual who is so unfortunate as to get into the habit of holding race prejudice....[54]

I have spoken of my admiration for General Armstrong, and yet he was but a type of that Christlike body of men and women who went into the Negro schools at the close of the war by the hundreds to assist in lifting up my race. The history of the world fails to show a higher, purer, and more unselfish class of men and women than those who found their way into those Negro schools....

No race can prosper till it learns that there is as much dignity in tilling a field as in writing a poem. [55]

Booker T. Washington stated:

I have always had the greatest respect for the work of The Salvation Army, especially because I have noted that draws no color line in religion. [56]

The Hon. John D. Long, Secretary of the Navy, spoke in honor of Booker T. Washington and his work at Tuskegee:

I cannot make a speech to-day. My heart is too full—full of hope, admiration, and pride for my countrymen of both sections and both colours. I am filled with gratitude and admiration for your work, and from this time forward I shall have absolute confidence in your progress and in the solution of the problem in which you are engaged.

The problem, I say, has been solved. A picture has been presented to-day which should be put upon canvas with the pictures of Washington and Lincoln, and transmitted to future time and generations—a picture which the press of the country should spread broadcast over the land, a most dramatic picture, and that picture is this: The President of the United States standing on this platform; on one side the Governor of Alabama, on the other, completing the trinity, a representative of a race only a few years ago in bondage, the coloured President of the Tuskegee Normal and Industrial Institute.

God bless the President under whose majesty such a scene as that is presented to the American people. God bless the state of Alabama, which is showing that it can deal with this problem for itself. God bless the orator, philanthropist, and disciple of the Great Master—who, if he were on earth, would be doing the same work—Booker T. Washington.

Author's Biographical Note

$\mathbf{T}$he first book I remember reading as a boy was on the life of George Washington Carver, given to me by my grandparents, Orval and Therese Epperson, affectionately known as "Poppy and Dede." Visiting their big house in Neosho, Missouri, every Easter was a highlight of our year. Often they would take us to the Carver Memorial in Diamond Grove, just 8 miles away.

In reading this book, *George Washington Carver – His Life & Faith in His Own Words,* I ask your indulgence in allowing me to give a glimpse of life in the small town of Neosho, where George lived and went to school as a young boy. Indeed, in a unique way, my childhood was touched by the same surroundings some ninety years later.

My grandfather, Orval, grew up not far away on a farm near the town of Anderson. The family had settled there in 1855 when his grandfather, George Washington Epperson, moved into the area from Tennessee, via Marion County, Illinois. At age fifteen, Orval, similar to Carver, left the farm and came to Neosho to pursue an education. He worked odd jobs around town to pay his tuition and eventually was hired by the cashier at the Bank of Neosho to serve as an assistant, run errands and sweep floors.

In 1918, he took a leave of absence to fight in France during World War I, being assigned to the 338th Machine Gun Battalion 88th Division. After the war, he returned to his job at the bank and worked there sixty-five years, becoming vice president. Everyone in Newton County knew him and before his retirement there was even declared an "Orval Epperson Day."

On July 4, 1919, Orval married Therese DeBrosse, "Dede," who had grown up in town of Monett. She moved to Neosho for employment and began working at the Neosho Nurseries at the edge of town. She was very beautiful, and we still have a turn-of-the-century advertisement featuring her selling canned peaches.

In this peaceful town, nicknamed "The Flower Box City," my grandfather never learned to drive a car, but instead would walk to work, walk back home for lunch - the big meal of the day - and again in the evening. Similar to George Carver, Orval was the epitome' of a green thumb, taking pride in the fact that no matter what season it was, some plant was blooming in his yard. My grandmother's nickname for my grandfather was, "Mr. Peaceful."

My grandparent's dream of a home came true when they purchased 344 South Hamilton, a large white house on several acres just up McKinney Street from the famous Missouri Fish Hatchery. The two story house had twelve-foot ceilings, walnut banisters up the stairs and large sliding doors between rooms. In the late 1800's, two prominent lawyers were competing to see who could build the best house. My grandparents home was one, and the home of artist Thomas Hart Benton, up the hill, was the other.

During the Great Depression and World War II, my grandparents responded to the needs of the community by allowing the soldiers stationed at Camp Crowder and their wives to live in their house. Each family dwelt in a separate room and shared the bathroom down the hall. For years, up to eighteen people lived in that house. Every morning, rain or snow, my grandparents would use an outside door from their bedroom and walk around the outside of the house to the kitchen, so as not to disturb the couples occupying the living and dining rooms. A large upstairs closet was the temporary home for a young woman from St. Louis and her husband from France. For several years there were numerous trailer homes all over their yard, and my grandfather even installed a bath and laundry machine in the basement for these tenants to use.

My grandparents had only one son, Billy. He was a "straight A" student and an Eagle Scout. When World War II started, he volunteered and was assigned as a bombardier in a B-17 Flying Fortress. On their last flight over Neosho before heading out to England, Billy wrote a note to my grandparents, tied it in a handkerchief and dropped in from the plane. A neighbor got it and brought to them. That was the closest my grandparents would ever be to him again, as Billy was shot down by the Nazis in his first mission over France. As his official listing was "Missing in Action," my grandparents prayed for years for him to be found, but when the war ended, their hearts were broken as word never came. They put a gravestone for him in the Neosho cemetery.

My grandparent's older daughter was Joan, who was beautiful, intelligent, and voted Neosho's "Centennial Queen." She worked for an advertising agency in New York and eventually moved to California, having married Jim Giles, later president of American Cement Company and board member of several banks. She received her Ph.D. in English and taught at Claremont College along with Jim, who was head of the Finance Department.

In the 1926, my grandmother, Dede, saw MGM's epic silent motion picture "Ben Hur: A Tale of the Christ," written by Civil War General Lew Wallace. She was so impressed she decided to name their last child, my mother, after the sister of Ben Hur, "Tirzah." My mother was gorgeous and during the war had every soldier at the USO hall wanting to dance with her. She broke many hearts, refusing marriage offers by the score. She moved to Washington, D.C., to work for the Department of Navy and later as junior executive at Kahn's Department Store. My father, Richard Federer, would drive from St. Louis to Washington to court her, then to Neosho to visit her parents, but that is another story.

My parents were married at St. Canera's, a little church on a hill overlooking Neosho's town square. The evening before the wedding, they went into the field and gathered daises for the altar of the church. My parents went on to have eleven children, of which I am fifth.

We looked forward to the long trip down the two-lane Highway 66 from St. Louis to Carthage, then south to Neosho, holding our breath as father would pull into the passing lane to pass those slow eighteen wheeler trucks which backed up traffic for miles on every hill. When entering the small town after dark and approaching my grandparents warm, loving home, we would always find the porch light left on for us.

Often, Poppy, my grandfather, would take us to work with him. Walking down the big hill of Lafayette Street, which my mother claimed was great to sled down in the winter, we would walk through the town square, by the oldest hotel, the nickel & dime store, the city hall, and make our way to the Bank of Neosho.

One summer, I had the fond experience of spending several weeks alone with my grandparents in Neosho. I remember riding the bicycle they bought for me across every hill and creek in town, from the railroad tracks to Big Spring Park, collecting one of every kind of leaf I could find. My grandfather would carefully examine each one, identifying it for me as I taped it in my scrap book. I can not help but think that much of the town I explored was the same as when George Washington Carver lived there as a boy.

Many times we would go to the George Washington Carver Memorial in Diamond Grove. We would see the movie of his life, study the replica of the cabin where Moses and Susan Carver raised George and his brother Jim, and explore the surrounding fields. We would stare at the tree where "Uncle Mose" Carver was hung up by his thumbs by the raiders that fateful night when George and his mother were kidnapped. We would hike through the woods and imagine young George touching the tiny plants and flowers, knowing someday he would touch the world.

Several years ago I had the honor of being the keynote speaker at the Officer Candidate School Graduation Formal at Fort Benning, Georgia. In meeting the new officers, I spent time visiting with Second Lieutenant McDaniel and his father, Willie, who was an employee of Tuskegee University. He extended an invitation for me to visit the campus, which I did on my trip home. My long desire was fulfilled of seeing the actual buildings where George Washington Carver and Booker T. Washington lived and worked.

Much like visiting a secret garden, the life of George Washington Carver holds mystery and inspiration, as the quiet woods beckon one to come deeper. The secret of his life bearing such great fruit seems to be rooted in his quiet, intimate relationship with his Creator. By reading his own words in these letters, we get a glimpse into the humble heart of this outstanding man, and perhaps discover keys to life's great accomplishments.

Over the years I have had the privilege of speaking across America, on radio, television, CSPAN, at colleges and universities, from the National Lawyers Association to the U.S. House Conference Committee. I had the honor of becoming friends with many great African American leaders, who mirror the spirit of George Washington Carver, rising from humble beginnings to impacting the world. They, like Carver, inspire us to "work on projects which fulfilled a real human need."

I am grateful to my grandparents for introducing me to the life of George Washington Carver, and I am thankful to you for allowing me the opportunity of exploring the life and faith of George Washington Carver with you.

My grandparents, Orval and Therese Epperson, of Neosho, Missouri
(1891-1976), (1893-1991)

ENDNOTES

1. Washington, Booker T. 1896, letter from Booker T. Washington, president of Tuskegee Institute, Tuskegee, Alabama to George Washington Carver. Dave Collins, George Washington Carver - Man's Slave becomes God's Scientist (Milford, MI: Mott Media, Inc., 1981), p. 66.

2. Carver, George Washington. May 16, 1896, in a letter to Booker T. Washington, president of Tuskegee Institute, Tuskegee, Alabama. Tuskegee Institute Archives, George Washington Carver Papers, reel 1, frame 0768. Gary R. Kremer, George Washington Carver - In His Own Words (Columbia, MO: University of Missouri Press, 1987), pp. 63-64.

3. Carver, George Washington. 1890c, in a letter to John and Helen Milholland, while he was a student at Simpson College. George Washington Carver National Monument, catalogue number 1484. Gary R. Kremer, George Washington Carver - In His Own Words (Columbia, Missouri: University of Missouri Press, 1987), p. 44.

4. Carver, George Washington. April 8, 1890, in a letter to John and Helen Milholland, while he was a student at Simpson College. George Washington Carver National Monument, catalogue number 1483. Gary R. Kremer, George Washington Carver - In His Own Words (Columbia, Missouri: University of Missouri Press, 1987), p. 45.

5. Carver, George Washington. August 6, 1891, in his first letter to John and Helen Milhollands after enrolling at Iowa State College in Ames, Iowa. George Washington Carver National Monument, catalogue number 1480. Gary R. Kremer, George Washington Carver - In His Own Words (Columbia, Missouri: University of Missouri Press, 1987), pp. 45-46.

6. Carver, George Washington. October 15, 1894, in a letter to John and Helen Milholland from Iowa State College, Ames, Iowa. George Washington Carver National Monument, catalogue number 1432. Gary R. Kremer, George Washington Carver - In His Own Words (Columbia, Missouri: University of Missouri Press, 1987), pp. 46-47.

7. Washington, Booker T. 1896, letter from Booker T. Washington, president of Tuskegee Institute, Tuskegee, Alabama to George Washington Carver. Dave Collins, George Washington Carver - Man's Slave becomes God's Scientist (Milford, MI: Mott Media, Inc., 1981), p. 66.

8. Carver, George Washington. May 16, 1896, in a letter to Booker T. Washington, president of Tuskegee Institute, Tuskegee, Alabama. Tuskegee Institute Archives, George Washington Carver Papers, reel 1, frame 0768. Gary R. Kremer, George Washington Carver - In His Own Words (Columbia, MO: University of Missouri Press, 1987), pp. 63-64.

9. Carver, George Washington. 1897, in a letter to two former professors, Mrs. Liston and Miss Budd. Tuskegee Institute Archives, George Washington Carver Papers, reel 1, frames 0001-6. Gary R. Kremer, George Washington Carver - In His Own Words (Columbia, MO: University of Missouri Press, 1987), p. 20-22.ress, 1987), pp. 20-22.

10. Carver, George Washington. September 2, 1901, in a letter from Tuskegee, Alabama to John and Helen Milholland. George Washington Carver National Monument, catalogue number 1444. Gary R. Kremer, George Washington Carver -

Endnotes

In His Own Words (Columbia, Missouri: University of Missouri Press, 1987), pp. 47-48.

11. Carver, George Washington. November 28, 1902, in a letter to the President of Tuskegee Institute, Booker T. Washington, regarding an unfortunate incident that resulted from the appearance of a white photographer, Frances B. Johnston, traveling the south with a black teacher, Nelson E. Henry, gathering information on black schools. Gary R. Kremer, George Washington Carver - In His Own Words (Columbia, MO: University of Missouri Press, 1987) pp. 149-151.

12. Carver, George Washington. May 28, 1907, in a letter to Booker T. Washington. Original in the Booker T. Washington Center, LC, Copy Tuskegee Institute Archives, George Washington Carver Papers, reel 3, frames 1227. Gary R. Kremer, George Washington Carver - In His Own Words (Columbia, Missouri: University of Missouri Press, 1987), p. 134.

13. Carver, George Washington. December 23, 1914, in a letter to John and Helen Milholland. George Washington Carver National Monument, catalogue number 1474. Gary R. Kremer, George Washington Carver - In His Own Words (Columbia, MO: University of Missouri Press, 1987), p. 48.

14. Carver, George Washington. 1920, in speaking at Blue Ridge, North Carolina to the Young Men's Christian Association. Ethel Edwards, Carver of Tuskegee (Cincinnati, Ohio: Ethel Edwards & James T. Hardwick, a limited edition work compiled in part from over 300 personal letters written by Dr. Carver to James T. Hardwick between 1922-1937, available from the Carver Memorial in Locust Grove, Diamond, MO., 1971), pp. 114-117.

15. Carver, George Washington. 1920, in speaking at Blue Ridge, North Carolina to the Young Men's Christian Association. Ethel Edwards, Carver of Tuskegee (Cincinnati, Ohio: Ethel Edwards & James T. Hardwick, a limited edition work compiled in part from over 300 personal letters written by Dr. Carver to James T. Hardwick between 1922-1937, available from the Carver Memorial in Locust Grove, Diamond, Mo., 1971), pp. 114-117.

16. Carver, George Washington. January 21, 1921, in addressing the House Ways and Means Committee in Washington, D.C. at the request of the United Peanut Growers Association, regarding a proposed tariff on imported peanuts. Hearings before the Committee on Ways and Means, House of Representatives on Schedule G, Agricultural Products and Provisions, January 21, 1921, Tariff Information, 1921 (Washington, 1921), pp. 1543-51. Copy Tuskegee Institute Archives, George Washington Carver Papers, reel 46, frames 0889-95. (Congress passed the Fordney Emergency Tariff Bill, which President Woodrow Wilson vetoed on March 3, 1921; President Calvin Coolidge signed the Emergency Tariff Act on May 27, 1921.) Gary R. Kremer, George Washington Carver - In His Own Words (Columbia, MO: University of Missouri Press, 1987), p. 112.

17. Carver, George Washington. January 21, 1921, in an address before the House Ways and Means Committee. Charles E. Jones, The Books You Read (Harrisburg, PA: Executive Books, 1985), p. 132.

18. Carver, George Washington. June 11, 1921, in a letter his old professor from Iowa State College, Dr. L.H. Pammel. Iowa State University Archives, Copy, Tuskegee Institute Archives, George Washington Carver Papers, reel 6, frames 0712-13. Gary R. Kremer, George Washington Carver - In His Own Words Columbia,

MO: University of Missouri Press, 1987), pp. 49-50.

19. Carver, George Washington. January 9, 1922, in a thank you note to one of his students, Mr. L. Robinson. Tuskegee Institute Archives, George Washington Carver Papers, reel 6, frame 1000. Gary R. Kremer, George Washington Carver - In His Own Words (Columbia, MO: University of Missouri Press, 1987), p. 85.

20. Carver, George Washington. 1922, autobiographical sketch. Tuskegee Institute Archives, George Washington Carver Papers, reel 1, frames 0011-14. Gary R. Kremer, George Washington Carver - In His Own Words (Columbia, MO: University of Missouri Press, 1987), p. 23-25.

21. Carver, George Washington. May 5, 1922, in a letter his old professor from Iowa State College, Dr. L.H. Pammel. Iowa State University Archives, Copy, Tuskegee Institute Archives, George Washington Carver Papers, reel 6, frames 1247-51. Gary R. Kremer, George Washington Carver - In His Own Words (Columbia, MO: University of Missouri Press, 1987), pp. 51-53.

22. Carver, George Washington. September 3, 1922, in a letter to Mrs. Helen Milholland. George Washington Carver National Monument, catalogue number 1426. Gary R. Kremer, George Washington Carver - In His Own Words (Columbia, Missouri: University of Missouri Press, 1987), p. 26.

23. Carver, George Washington. September 17, 1922, in a letter to Mrs. Helen Milholland. George Washington Carver National Monument, catalogue number 1456. Gary R. Kremer, George Washington Carver - In His Own Words (Columbia, Missouri: University of Missouri Press, 1987), p. 26.

24. Carver, George Washington. Statement made in conversation with James Hardwick, Ethel Edwards, Carver of Tuskegee, pp. 119-122. James Hardwick wrote the foreword for Edwards' book, stating "Ethel Edwards has portrayed the man I knew and loved better than any other writer." Gary R. Kremer, George Washington Carver - In His Own Words (Columbia, Missouri: University of Missouri Press, 1987), p. 14.

25. Carver, George Washington. Henry A. Wallace, U.S Secretary of Agriculture and Vice-President under Franklin D. Roosevelt described George Washington Carver in a letter to Luzanne Boozer, December 7, 1948, quoted in McMurry, George Washington Carver, p. 41. Gary R. Kremer, George Washington Carver - In His Own Words (Columbia, Missouri: University of Missouri Press, 1987), p. 59.

26. Carver, George Washington. January 6, 1924, in a letter to his former Professor, U.S. Secretary of Agriculture Henry C. Wallace. National Archives, Record Group 16, Copy, Tuskegee Institute Archives, George Washington Carver Papers, reel 7, frame 0752. Gary R. Kremer, George Washington Carver - In His Own Words (Columbia, MO: University of Missouri Press, 1987), p. 59.

27. Carver, George Washington. May 21, 1924, in a letter to James T. Hardwick. Tuskegee Institute Archives, George Washington Carver Papers, reel 39, frame 1069. Gary R. Kremer, George Washington Carver - In His Own Words (Columbia, Missouri: University of Missouri Press, 1987), pp. 37-38.

28. Carver, George Washington. July 10, 1924, in a letter to Mr. James T. "Jimmie" Hardwick of Virginia. Tuskegee Institute Archives, George Washington Carver Papers, reel 8, frames 0045-47. Gary R. Kremer, George Washington Carver - In His Own Words (Columbia, Missouri: University of Missouri Press, 1987), pp. 138-139.

Endnotes

29. Carver, George Washington. November 19, 1924, in a speech before 500 people of the Women's Board of Domestic Missions in New York City's Marble Collegiate Church. Ethel Edwards, Carver of Tuskegee (Cincinnati, OH: Ethel Edwards & James T. Hardwick, a limited edition work compiled in part from over 300 personal letters written by Dr. Carver to James T. Hardwick between 1922-1937, from Carver Memorial, Locust Grove, Diamond, MO., 1971), pp. 141-142.

30. Carver, George Washington. Ethel Edwards, Carver of Tuskegee (Cincinnati, OH: Ethel Edwards & James T. Hardwick, a limited edition work compiled in part from over 300 personal letters written by Dr. Carver to James T. Hardwick between 1922-1937, available from the Carver Memorial in Locust Grove, Diamond, MO., 1971), pp. 183, 199.

31. Carver, George Washington. November 24, 1924, in a letter to the editor of the New York Times, correcting an editorial they ran entitled "Men of Science Never Talk that Way," in which they attempted to discredit Carver, his race and Tuskegee Institute. Tuskegee Institute Archives, George Washington Carver Papers, reel 8, frame 0444-45. Gary R. Kremer, George Washington Carver - In His Own Words (Columbia, Missouri: University of Missouri Press, 1987), pp. 129-130.

32. Carver, George Washington. January 15, 1925, in a letter to the Rev. Lyman Ward, founder of an industrial school in Camp Hill, Alabama. Original in the possession of Mrs. Crawford A. Rose, Providence, Louisiana, Copy, Tuskegee Institute Archives, George Washington Carver Papers, reel 8, frames 0772-73. Gary R. Kremer, George Washington Carver - In His Own Words (Columbia, Missouri: University of Missouri Press, 1987), pp. 130-131.

33. Carver, George Washington. March 24, 1925, in a letter to Robert Johnson, an employee of Chesley Enterprises of Ontario. Tuskegee Institute Archives, George Washington Carver Papers, reel 8, frames 1032-33. Gary R. Kremer, George Washington Carver - In His Own Words (Columbia, Missouri: University of Missouri Press, 1987), pp. 131-133.

34. Carver, George Washington. March 24, 1925, in a letter to Rev. Kunzman of Seattle. Tuskegee Institute Archives, George Washington Carver Papers, reel 8, frames 1034. Gary R. Kremer, George Washington Carver - In His Own Words (Columbia, Missouri: University of Missouri Press, 1987), p. 133.

35. Carver, George Washington. March 1, 1927, in a letter to Jack Boyd, a YMCA official in Denver, Colorado. Tuskegee Institute Archives, George Washington Carver Papers, reel 10, frames 0635-37. Gary R. Kremer, George Washington Carver - In His Own Words (Columbia, Missouri: University of Missouri Press, 1987), pp. 134-135.

36. Carver, George Washington. December 13, 1927, in a letter to the Hon. Leon McCord, circuit court judge, 15th Judicial District, Montgomery, AL. Tuskegee Institute Archives, George Washington Carver Papers, reel 10, frames 0946-47. Gary R. Kremer, George Washington Carver - In His Own Words (Columbia, MO: University of Missouri Press, 1987), pp. 136-137.

37. Carver, George Washington. 1928, Tuskegee Institute. Ethel Edwards, Carver of Tuskegee (Cincinnati, OH: Ethel Edwards & James T. Hardwick, a limited edition work compiled in part from over 300 personal letters written by Dr. Carver to James T. Hardwick between 1922-1937, available at Carver Memorial, Locust Grove, Diamond, MO., 1971), pp. 157-160.

38. Carver, George Washington. January 25, 1929, in a letter to Mrs. Eva Goodwin in Neosho, Missouri. She was the daughter of one of Carver's boyhood playmates, Thomas Williams, who was a great-nephew of Moses Carver. George Washington Carver National Monument, catalogue number 1390. Gary R. Kremer, George Washington Carver - In His Own Words (Columbia, Missouri: University of Missouri Press, 1987), pp. 40-41.

39. Carver, George Washington. February 24, 1930, in a letter to Hubert W. Pelt of the Phelps Stokes Fund, in which he included a brief essay entitled "How to Search for Truth". Tuskegee Institute Archives, George Washington Carver Papers, reel 12, frames 0029-32. Gary R. Kremer, George Washington Carver - In His Own Words (Columbia, Missouri: University of Missouri Press, 1987), pp. 142-143.

40. Carver, George Washington. July 24, 1931, in a letter to Miss Isabelle Coleman of Greensboro, NC. National Archives, Record Group 16, Copy, Tuskegee Institute Archives, George Washington Carver Papers, reel 12, frames 1264-65. Gary R. Kremer, George Washington Carver - In His Own Words (Columbia, MO: University of Missouri Press, 1987), pp. 127-128.

41. Carver, George Washington. March 1, 1932, in a letter to Mr. Zissler. Original in the Iowa State University Archives, Copy, Tuskegee Institute Archives, George Washington Carver Papers, reel 13, frames 0395. Gary R. Kremer, George Washington Carver - In His Own Words (Columbia, Missouri: University of Missouri Press, 1987), pp. 137-138.

42. Carver, George Washington. July 1, 1932, in a letter to Mr. James T. "Jimmie" Hardwick of Virginia. Tuskegee Institute Archives, George Washington Carver Papers, reel 13, frames 0531. Gary R. Kremer, George Washington Carver - In His Own Words (Columbia, Missouri: University of Missouri Press, 1987), p. 140.

43. Carver, George Washington. December 16, 1934, in a letter to the mother of Mr. James T. "Jimmie" Hardwick. George Washington Carver National Monument, catalogue number 537. Gary R. Kremer, George Washington Carver - In His Own Words (Columbia, Missouri: University of Missouri Press, 1987), pp. 145-146.

44. Carver, George Washington. March 15, 1935, in a letter to the Rev. Thomas O. Parish of Topeka, Kansas. George Washington Carver National Monument, catalogue number 491. Gary R. Kremer, George Washington Carver - In His Own Words (Columbia, Missouri: University of Missouri Press, 1987), p. 144.

45. Carver, George Washington. March 22, 1935, in a letter to the mother of Mrs. James T. "Jimmie" Hardwick. George Washington Carver National Monument, catalogue number 535. Gary R. Kremer, George Washington Carver - In His Own Words (Columbia, Missouri: University of Missouri Press, 1987), p. 146.

46. Carver, George Washington. September 30, 1935, ion a letter to the Rev. Thomas O. Parrish of Topeka, Kansas. George Washington Carver National Monument, catalogue number 492. Gary R. Kremer, George Washington Carver - In His Own Words (Columbia, Missouri: University of Missouri Press, 1987), pp. 144-145.

47. Carver, George Washington. March 17, 1937, letter to the editor of Roanoke, AL, Leader, Mr. Stevenson, whose son he had treated for paralysis. Tuskegee Institute Archives, George Washington Carver Papers, reel 20, frames 0819-20. Gary R. Kremer, George Washington Carver - In His Own Words (Columbia, MO: University of Missouri Press, 1987), pp. 133-134.

48. Carver, George Washington. January 28, 1938, in correspondence to Harry O.

Abbott, who served as his traveling secretary. George Washington Carver National Monument, catalogue number 395. Gary R. Kremer, George Washington Carver - In His Own Words (Columbia, Missouri: University of Missouri Press, 1987), pp. 81-82.

49. Carver, George Washington. August 24, 1940, in a letter to a Tuskegee minister, Rev. Haygood. Tuskegee Institute Archives, George Washington Carver Papers, reel 34, frames 1097. Gary R. Kremer, George Washington Carver - In His Own Words (Columbia, Missouri: University of Missouri Press, 1987), p. 136.

50. Carver, George Washington. September 7, 1940, in a letter to Mr. and Mrs. Woods. Tuskegee Institute Archives, George Washington Carver Papers, reel 35, frames 0066. Gary R. Kremer, George Washington Carver - In His Own Words (Columbia, Missouri: University of Missouri Press, 1987), pp. 140-141.

51. Carver, George Washington. December 16, 1941, in a letter to the Rev. Carl A. Blackman of Kansas City, Missouri. Tuskegee Institute Archives, George Washington Carver Papers, reel 39, frames 0513. Gary R. Kremer, George Washington Carver - In His Own Words (Columbia, Missouri: University of Missouri Press, 1987), p. 141.

52. Carver, George Washington. Bless Your Heart (series II) (Eden Prairie, MN: Heartland Samplers, Inc., 1990), 7.12.

53. Carver, George Washington. 1939, in the citation made at the presentation of the Roosevelt Medal. Henry M. Morris, Men of Science - Men of God (El Cajon, CA: Master Books, Creation Life Publishers, Inc., 1990), pp. 81-83.

54. Washington, Booker Taliaferro. Bob Cutshall, More Light for the Day (Minneapolis, MN: Northwestern Products, Inc., 1991), 1.20. Perry Tanksley, To Love is to Give (Jackson, Mississippi: Allgood Books, Box 1329; Parthenon Press, 201 8th Ave., South, Nashville, Tennessee, 1972), p. 43.

55. Washington, Booker Taliaferro. Perry Tanksley, To Love is to Give (Jackson, MS: Allgood Books, Box 1329; Parthenon Press, 201 8th Ave., South, Nashville, TN, 1972), p. 51.

56. Washington, Booker Taliaferro. Kevin A. Miller, "Fashionable or Forceful" (Carol Stream, IL: Christian History, 465 Gunderson Drive, Carol Stream, IL 60188, 1990), Issue 26, Volume IX, No. 2, p. 2.

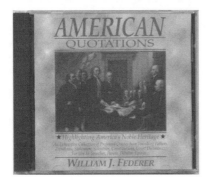